Redeemed
But Who Am I?

By Angela Lougee

Redeemed
But Who Am I?

By Angela Lougee

Rhema Solutions Today Ministries
P.O. Box 133
Peck, Idaho 83545
USA

Redeemed
But Who Am I?

Copyright © 2024 by Angela Lougee

All rights are reserved solely by the author. The author guarantees all contents are original and do not infringe upon the legal rights of any other person or work. No part of this book may be reproduced without the author's permission except for brief quotations in critical reviews or articles.

Unless otherwise indicated, Bible quotations are taken from HEBREW GREEK KEY WORD STUDY BIBLE, NEW INTERNATIONAL VERSION OF THE BIBLE. Copyright © 1996 by AMG International, Inc. Used by permission.

Scripture quotations marked (NKJV) are taken from the New King James Version Copyright © 1982 by Thomas Nelson, Inc. Used by permission. All rights reserved.

Scripture quotations marked (TLB) are taken from The Living Bible copyright © 1971. Used by permission of Tyndale House Publishers, Carol Stream, Illinois 60188. All rights reserved.

Scripture quotations marked (ESV) are taken from THE HOLY BIBLE, ENGLISH STANDARD VERSION®, Copyright© 2001 by Crossway, a publishing ministry of Good News Publishers. Used by permission. All rights reserved.

Scripture quotations marked NASB95 are taken from the New American Standard Bible (1995 Update) Copyright © 1981, 1998 THE LOCKMAN FOUNDATION. Used by permission. All rights reserved.

Scripture quotations marked KJV are taken from King James Version Database © 2006 WORDsearch Corp. All rights reserved.

Any trademarks mentioned are the property of their respective owners.

All rights reserved. This book is protected by the copyright laws of the United States of America. This book may not be copied or reprinted for commercial gain or profit. The use of short quotations or occasional page copying for personal, or group study is permitted and encouraged. Permission will be granted upon request.

Requests for bulk sales discounts, editorial permissions, or other information should be addressed to:

Scroll Publishers
PO Box 5847
Pinehurst, NC 28374 USA

Additional copies available at www.scrollpublishers.com

ISBN 13 TP: 978-1-962808-04-0

ISBN 13 eBook: 978-1-962808-05-7

Cover Design by Darian Horner Design
(www.darianhorner.com)
Image: 123rf.com #105958628

First Edition: July 2024

10 9 8 7 6 5 4 3 2 1 0

Printed in the United States of America

Download The Audiobook Free

Thank you for purchasing my book. As a token of my appreciation, I'm excited to offer you the audiobook version free. You're more likely to enjoy and complete this book with the audiobook version. I narrated it, so it feels like a heartfelt conversation between us. Instead of paying $10-$20, I'm thrilled to gift it to you for free.

ANGELALOUGEE.COM/AUDIOBOOK

Take Your Journey Further With Our Companion Workbook

Download the digital version now at angelalougee.com and deepen your self-discovery and growth. Embrace this inspiring resource and unlock your true potential.

Instead of paying $10, download it for free as my gift to you.

ANGELALOUGEE.COM/FREEWORKBOOK

Table of Contents

Dedication i

Thank You iii

Foreword v

Preface vii

Chapter One
    The Heavenly Realms and Our Beginning 1

Chapter Two
    The Redeemed as a Reflection of the Godhead 9

Chapter Three
    The Redeemed as the Bride of Christ 15

Chapter Four
    The Redeemed as God's Living Mobile Home 31

Chapter Five
    The Redeemed as Different Types of Houses 45

Chapter Six
    The Redeemed
    as Authorized Agents to Cast Out Demons 57

Chapter Seven
  The Redeemed
  Process of Becoming a Residence for the Godhead....81

Chapter Eight
  The Redeemed as Co-Laborers..95

Chapter Nine
  The Redeemed as God's Field..109

Chapter Ten
  The Redeemed as Intercessors.......................................117

Chapter Eleven
  Approaching God as Judge..129

Chapter Twelve
  The Redeemed
  as the Most Resourced Beings on Earth......................151

Chapter Thirteen
  The Redeemed
  as a Praiser and a Hallelujah-Raiser.............................155

Chapter Fourteen
  Redeemed, But Who Am I?..163

Description... 169

About the Author...171

Dedication

To Yahweh, our Heavenly Father, Living Word Yeshua, and Spirit of Holiness, I am forever in awe of you. I lack the words to express the depth of my gratitude for who You are and all You do. Thank You!

To our daughter Jedidiah, you are a joy to have. We are honored that Papa Yahweh chose your dad and me as your earthly parents.

Thank You

Pastors Bill Courtnay, David Pepper, and Brad Wuori; thank you for reading through this manuscript. Your feedback was priceless! May the Lord reward your kindness.

To my husband, Michael, thank you for your love and support. You are a blessing beyond measure!

To my mom, there are no words to express the depth of my gratitude for the gift of having you as my mom. Your love, self-control, tenacity, and dedication are inspirational!

To all the saints who have sowed in various ways into my life, thank you for your obedience to the Lord.

Ari, thank you for your editing skills. You are a blessing on the Earth!

Dr. Ron Horner and the LifeSpring International Ministries team, you have enriched my life. Thank you!

Foreword

Understanding who you are in the Kingdom of God is central to every follower of Christ living their best life now. Through the lens of redemption, Angela Lougee mines truth from the scriptures that is clear, balanced, and thought-provoking. When you read the stories of her journey, you will be inspired in life-changing ways to be the masterpiece God has redeemed you to be. Angela herself is a brilliant speaker, bold yet sweet, with an enthusiastic, genuine spirit that blesses many. I recall the first time I saw her in a church service, praising and worshipping in a way that reflected her love for God and her authentic demonstration that he loved her. Her contagious, effervescent personality, as well as her humble confidence in being a daughter of God, overflows into the words of this book. Having planted Church on the Rock in Wasilla, Alaska, and now leading an organization in the Amazon jungle that makes disciples, I have witnessed how this issue of identity is so vital for individuals worldwide who have come to faith in Jesus

Christ. Knowing who you are and who you are not as a Christian is a message the Church needs to hear today.

David Pepper
President of Amazon Outreach

Preface

At conception, each of us embarked on a journey through time. If we live long enough, we will ask two questions embedded in every human: who am I, and why am I here on Earth?

I believe that our Creator placed within us a desire to know the answers to these questions from when we left His loins and showed up in our mother's womb. By God's design, we have a deep longing to understand our origin and purpose so that we will be drawn to Him, the source of our identity (Acts 17:26-28). Those who search and gain understanding will enjoy a more fulfilling and passionate existence if they follow the path of their findings.

> *From one man, he made every nation of men, that they should inhabit the whole Earth, and he determined the times set for them and the exact places where they should live. God did this so that men would seek him and perhaps reach out for him and find him, though he is not far from each one of us. 'For in him we live*

> *and move and have our being.' As some of your own poets have said, 'We are his offspring.'* (Acts 17:26-28)

The sooner we come to a clear conclusion about our identity and align ourselves with our life's purpose, the more satisfying and peaceful the remainder of our voyage through time will be. Note, however, that peace is not the absence of turbulence but the presence of a person—Jesus Christ. He assures us, amid a raging storm, that victory is ours regardless of the circumstance.

In *Redeemed, But Who Am I?*, I am inviting you on a life-changing discovery path that leads to a revelation of who you are as the redeemed on Earth. I'll get into precisely what that means soon, but first, let me say that I am thankful that our Heavenly Father did not leave us clueless. Our generation has access to the 66 books of the Bible that collectively serve as a road map to our divine purpose. This access is a privilege that many past generations were not granted. Consider that Noah, Abraham, David, Paul, and Peter did not have all 66 books at their disposal. Considering that, we must always be mindful of how blessed we are to have been given so much. Let us run our race and remember, that to whom much is given, God will expect much.

> *But he that knew not and did commit things worthy of stripes shall be beaten with few*

> stripes. For unto whomsoever much is given, of him shall be much required: and to whom men have committed much, of him they will ask the more. Luke 12:48 (KJV)

Another honor we have, which we do share with our biblical heroes, is existing in the realm of time. Do you realize that not every Heavenly being has participated in God's time system governing the Earth? In Heaven, there is no such thing as time as we know it. Heaven does not run on a 24-hour daily cycle. The Bible says to God, one day is like a thousand years (2 Peter 3:8).

> *But do not forget this one thing, dear friends: With the Lord, a day is like a thousand years, and a thousand years are like a day.* (2 Peter 3:8)

Things function differently in our world, and all the beings in Heaven know about our unique universe. They hear and read about us, and they long to discover even more about our redemption (1 Peter 1:12). Only those whose assignment brings them here come to Earth. Some are assigned only to the heavens, and others, while staying occupied in the heavens, are waiting for their time to be sent to Earth.

> *It was revealed to them that they were not serving themselves but you, when they spoke of the things that have now been told you by those who have preached the gospel to you by the Holy Spirit sent from Heaven. Even angels long to look into these things.* (1 Peter 1:12)

As you read the pages of this book, I pray that your passion will be awakened, your hunger to know our Redeemer will increase, and your desire to be all God created you to be will intensify. It is also my hope that you will learn what it means to be counted among the Redeemed and be filled with endless joy and gratitude that our Heavenly Father chose you to participate in the realm of time.

Chapter One

The Heavenly Realms and Our Beginning

Suppose you have read the first page of the Bible. In that case, you are familiar with the opening phrase of Genesis 1:1: "In the beginning, God created the heavens and the earth."

When I was 13, I remember lying in bed, trying to make sense of that exact verse. I asked God two questions: If You created the heavens and the Earth in the beginning, where were You before the beginning? If nothing existed before You created the heavens and the Earth, were you living in nothingness?

Being curious by nature, I have asked the Lord many similar things. When I read the Bible, my vivid imagination goes to work. It feels like I am simultaneously stepping into a movie theater and onto a film set. I don't just watch what is shown to me but also think about what is happening behind the scenes.

Reading Scriptures with this level of curiosity generates a lot of questions in me.

I am glad we have been given the Holy Spirit as our teacher; I usually direct all my queries to Him. Although I don't always get immediate responses, I eventually receive them, even if it takes days, weeks, months, or years. I believe God keeps an actual record of what I ask Him because when the answer shows up, He makes it a point to remind me of what I previously requested.

For instance, I did not get feedback regarding the questions sparked by Genesis 1:1 for quite some time. Then, one day, it dawned on me. Isaiah 66:1 and Matthew 5:34 were highlighted for me. Both the Father and the Son confirm that Heaven is God's throne in these two passages. It made sense that God lived in His palace before He created the heavens and Earth. Being born into a royal family, I know a king's throne occupies only a portion of His palace. My brain made this association because I was raised in a nation with kingdoms. I have also visited palaces with many throne rooms, and I know that wherever the king sits, that becomes a throne room for the moment.

The king makes the throne; the throne does not make the king. Special throne rooms were built in every palace for specific occasions.

As I was reading through the Scriptures, I noticed that palaces on Earth are somewhat patterned after God's palace in the spirit realm. As I mentioned, Earthly palaces typically have multiple rooms and designated areas. Some spaces are for common use, whereas others can only be accessed by invitation. In John 14:2, Jesus told His disciples that there are many rooms in His Father's house. The word rooms, in English, translates as mansions, dwelling places, lodgings, abodes, homes, and resting places. It is also the word for habitation. Jesus was letting us know that there are many realms in His Father's palace. The heavens mentioned in Genesis 1:1 are just one of the Heavenly realms in God's palace. The whole of eternity is His palace. How great is our God!

Other Realms

Before Jesus, the Word became flesh and died for the redemption of mankind; when the righteous died, they went to a place the Bible calls paradise or Abraham's bosom (Luke 23:42-43). That, too, was one of the realms of our Heavenly Father's palace, and it was not a cheap place. We know this because the Bible says both Moses and Elijah "appeared in glorious splendor" on the Mount of Transfiguration with Jesus as they discussed His upcoming assignment (Luke 9:28-36). Unlike the righteous dead, the unrighteous dead are currently in one of three realms: the sea, death, or hell (Revelation 20:13). At the final judgment, anyone whose name is not written in the Book of Life will be cast into the lake of fire. The realms of hell and death will also be cast into the lake of fire (Revelation 20:14-15).

Lucifer and his cohorts, who were kicked out of Heaven before man was created, are only temporarily allowed to occupy one of the lower heavenly realms (Ephesians 6:12). However, when the fullness of time comes, they will all be cast down to Earth by Michael and his angels (Revelation 12:7-9). When that season is over, as determined by God's agenda, Satan and his legion will be thrown into the lake of fire by another angel (Revelation 20:10). The good news is that they will be there forever and ever.

Our Beginning

The beginning that is described in Genesis 1:1 was not the first beginning. There were other beginnings before that. For example, Scripture says that when God created wisdom, she was the first of God's creations (Proverbs 8:22-31).

Genesis 1:1 tells the story of time as we now know it and lays out the journey of mankind from creation to redemption and beyond.

Before our beginning, God already had an existing governmental system, complete with elders (Revelation 4:4), living creatures, angels, and Heavenly armies. Though the kingdom of Heaven was already functioning, God was not satisfied. He wanted an even bigger family. Besides, after Lucifer and his cohorts were kicked out of God's Kingdom, there were vacancies for worshippers and priests (Ezekiel 28:11-16). Those newly open slots were to be filled with mankind (Revelation 1:6). Therefore, God started creation in eternity past and rested only after mankind was created (Genesis 2:3).

We existed in God before appearing in our mama's womb (Ephesians 1:4-6). He wrote and published a book about every one of us before we began our journey into time. All the days of our lives were written in that book before one of them ever came to pass (Psalm 139:16). When God began His creation project, He called it a good work (Philippians 1:6). Keeping this in mind, as we journey through time, even when we make mistakes, the debris from our falls and stumbles, once turned over to Him, become construction materials for His good work in progress (Romans 8:28).

The Glory Impact

The glory of God is the very essence of God. As it is in Heaven, God desires for the Earth to be marinated in the knowledge of His glory. Before man sinned, the Earth was so saturated with God's glory that green plants did not need the light of the sun to make their food. The radiance of God's glory defied science. How do we know this? Read the creation sequence in Genesis 1. You will see that God waited until after creating vegetation to make the sun and moon (Genesis 1:11-16).

Furthermore, during creation, the intensity of the glory was so strong that there was no room for darkness; God put it away (Genesis 1:3-5). Do you notice no more mention of darkness or night until after man sinned? There was evening and morning each day, but there was no night. Where was the night? God sent it to its residence (Job 38:19-20). It could not coexist with the level of glory that was present before the fall. Also, there will be no darkness or night on the promised new Earth. Scripture says lamps and sunlight will be unnecessary, too (Revelation 22:5). In the end, things will be the way God intended from the beginning—incomparably better!

It is worth noting there are different levels or intensities of God's glory. The best way to explain this is by using the lumens of a light bulb as an example. Lumens measure the brightness of a bulb. The higher the lumens, the brighter the light is. It is said that direct sunlight is around 100,000 lumens. Speaking of the brightness of light, I have one of those lamps with adjustable lighting in my living room. That means, with a simple turn of a knob, I can either make the bulb shine brighter or dimmer. Similarly, God can adjust the intensity of His glory and dim it to whatever level is tolerable to an individual, group, or situation.

From the beginning, God created mankind as a conduit through which all creation would experience His glory. Just like the knob on my lampstand can dim the lumens of a bulb, God can dim His glory. Man's relationship with Him determines the brightness or dimness of God's glory on Earth. When man fell, it can be said that the glory knob, if you will, was turned to its lowest position.

Scripture tells us that all have sinned and fallen short of the glory of God (Romans 3:23). When my living room lamp is dimmed, even though it has the capacity for much brighter lighting, the bulb emits a very low level of light. Likewise, though the Earth is filled with the glory of God (Isaiah 6:3), because the conduit, mankind, is either missing in action or has been taken as a prisoner of war by sin, the intensity of the glory is greatly lessened.

But make no mistake, God will have His way in this matter. The experiential knowledge of the glory of God will someday cover the Earth as the waters cover the sea (Habakkuk 2:14). When Jesus shed His blood and died on Calvary, He paid the total price for this to happen. When the Redeemed become mature enough to exercise their full rights as sons (Galatians 4:1-5), creation will again experience the level of glory they once knew before sin precipitated the fall (Romans 8:19-21).

In the beginning, we were created to know God, love Him, serve Him, and experience happiness dwelling in His glory—both in this life and the life to come. The more we know Him, the more we love Him. The more we love Him, the more we serve Him. The more we serve Him, the happier we are with Him, both now and forever. Our divine purpose is to host and reflect God's glory (John 17:22).

Chapter Two

The Redeemed as a Reflection of the Godhead

Everything God created first existed in God before the Word made it.

In Genesis, throughout the creation account, the word Elohim is used, the Hebrew word for God. Elohim is a plural form of God, which indicates the activity of the Godhead.

The Godhead comprises the Father, the Spirit, and the Word. In case you didn't know, Jesus' name was simply the Word before He became Jesus Christ (John 1:1, 14). We will use the two interchangeably in this book. In the biblical story of creation, the Holy Spirit was seen hovering over the surface of the waters (Genesis 1:2). In Genesis 1, the Father is speaking, the Son is doing, and the Spirit is revealing.

In Genesis 1:26, God, having created a habitable earth, declared it was time to form mankind. He also decided that humans would be fashioned in the image and likeness of the Godhead. Therefore, we were molded to reflect the outward and inward nature of the Godhead. Humankind is meant to look like God outwardly and act like Him too. In the Godhead, we observe a three-in-one phenomenon known as the Trinity or Triune nature of God. Just like the divine Trinity, mankind has a triune nature. We are spirit beings with souls who live in bodies. Our earthly body was made from the dust of the earth. Our spirit, however, came from God (Genesis 2:7).

Genesis 1:27 states that males and females were created to reflect God's image. One without the other is an incomplete representation of God's image and likeness. God has both male and female attributes. To me, He is not just my Father God but also my Mother God. As a redeemed woman, I reflect the image and likeness of the One who formed me.

Visible Likeness of the Invisible God

Hebrews 1:3 describes Jesus, the Son of Man, as the visible likeness of the invisible God. I can relate to that description because I have a daughter who is about to turn ten at the time of this writing. As I watch her behavior, I also see a visible likeness of the invisible me. She thinks and acts like the person I am inside; the only difference is she amplifies my unseen traits. I used to say if anyone wanted to see the hidden part of me, they just needed to observe my daughter. It melts my heart to watch her display my positive characteristics. She reflects my character in much the same way as I reflect the character of my Heavenly Father. Sometimes, when I correct her, I hear God chuckle and say, "Look who's talking. You're just like her!"

God was intentional about making us in His image and likeness. I bet, just like me, it melts His heart when He sees His children thinking and behaving like Him. I can only imagine the joy and awe the angels and all celestial beings experienced when Jesus was born. They got the chance to see a visible representation of the indescribable God. Jesus was a pure personification of the Father, untainted by sin. No wonder when Christ was born in Bethlehem, a great company of Heavenly hosts broke out singing, "Glory to God in the Highest" (Luke 2:13-14)!

Distorted at Birth

My special needs son moved back to Heaven three weeks before turning 17. He succumbed to complications following a bone marrow transplant that was performed to cure him of a disease. He was born with Sickle Cell Anemia. It is a blood disorder that both his dad and I passed along to him at conception because we were both born with a recessive sickle cell gene.

Whether or not you were born with health challenges, every single one of us was distorted and damaged in different ways at birth—some visible and others invisible. Unlike us, before the fall, Adam and Eve were created in the image and likeness of God (Genesis 1:27; 5:1-2). Every other person, except for Jesus Christ, was born in the image and likeness of fallen man—damaged (Genesis 5:3). After sin entered the world through Adam and Eve, none were born as initially intended by God. But here is the good news: when we are born again by accepting Jesus as our Savior and Lord, we become a new creation known as the Redeemed (2 Corinthians 5:17). At our rebirth, God's transforming power immediately starts working in us and conforming us into the likeness of Jesus Christ (Romans 8:29).

But understand that this transformational process does not happen overnight. We all begin as spiritual babies; over time, the more we eat, the hungrier we get, and the more we grow. When our diet is balanced—consisting of Bible study, fellowship, communion, and steadfast prayer—the healthier we become. As we are strengthened in our walk with God, we exercise our faith and become spiritually mature. We deepen our obedience to God and enjoy a more intimate relationship with Him.

Unique Manifestation

With the darkness we see today, have you ever wondered why God continues to gift us with babies? It's because He has so much of Himself that He yet wants to reveal through humankind! Science confirms that no other person shares your fingerprints or voice or the pattern of the iris inside your eye. Each of us represents a unique manifestation of God. When the angels look at the Redeemed, they see the visible likeness of the invisible God. Without observing us, there are attributes of the Father that the angels could never see. Don't you know you are a sign and a wonder to principalities and powers?

God teaches heavenly beings through the Redeemed about His multifaceted and multidimensional wisdom (Ephesians 3:10). You are valuable. There is only one of you in creation. You are God's masterpiece and deeply loved by the Father. To Heavenly beings, you are a reference point of God's wisdom.

Chapter Three

The Redeemed as the Bride of Christ

One time, I had a dream that I was caught up to Heaven and shown a book about the life of Martin Luther King, Jr. The most fascinating thing happened when I opened that book. It came alive as if I were watching a movie as I read it. Since I have no reference point for this on Earth, I call it a "video book." Our God is a genius!

As I told you earlier, God is a writer and publisher of books (Psalm 139:16). There is even a book about His Son, the Word, in the libraries of Heaven (Hebrews 10:7). The angels have access to these libraries, and they can read God's books to learn about His agenda and their assignments (Daniel 10:20). All the books in Heaven are living books. Can you imagine what the angels thought when they first read about how the Word would be made flesh, dwell among men, redeem them, and marry them? I bet this was a mystery that they could not wait to watch unfold. Can you see in your mind's eye their reaction when they read the memo or heard the news about the day God would begin creating the Earth?

Wow! Finally, they would behold mankind, a different being, with flesh made from dust. Better still, one day, the angels would be firsthand witnesses to Jesus appearing in the likeness of mankind and marrying them. The angels may have asked, what's a wedding? Remember, they had no reference point for such a thing because the Bible says that angels neither marry nor are given in marriage (Matthew 22:2-30). The story of mankind's redemption culminates in the wedding feast of the Lamb (Revelation 19:6-9). The marriage between the Lamb and His bride is a true happily-ever-after love story. Unlike on Earth, where death separates couples, the Lamb's marriage will never end.

Sometimes, I wonder if there were impatient angels. Did their eagerness to see all these events unfold drive them to behave like humans on a long road trip, asking, "When are we going to be there?" or "Are we there yet?" When God made Adam, all of Heaven saw for the first time what the Word would look like in the future. I can't wait to view Heaven's video books to observe Jesus' appearance before He became flesh. I am thankful for a record-keeping God!

The Bride Price

In most cultures outside the Western world, A groom must pay a bride price before a bride's family will give her to a groom. In some cultures, the bride's family pays the groom's dowry. In my country of birth, there are at least two phases in the marriage process: traditional and church weddings. Depending on a person's denomination, there can be a third phase known as the court wedding. In such instances, even if a couple weds at the court and the church, if they do not have the traditional wedding, they are not considered married by each tribal culture. Couples in my native country have at least two weddings to plan.

The traditional marriage typically begins with the groom's family approaching the family of the bride-to-be. They make it known that they are in search of a bride for their son. After a single visit—or multiple visits, depending on the tribe—if the groom is deemed agreeable by the bride's relatives, a date is set for the groom's family to return with a list of items, including the bride price.

The bride price, as well as other requirements, may vary. Sometimes, the more educated a girl is, the higher the cost. In some parts of the world, the bride price could be as expensive as USD 100,000. In my country of birth, the high cost of getting married led to fewer divorces.

Couples felt compelled to figure out ways to work things out due to the costliness of the union. Well, once the bride price is paid and accepted, the bride's father must hand the daughter to the groom for a traditional wedding ceremony. The nuptials include many elaborate festivities.

Back to the Garden

As the events in Genesis were revealed, the angels watched God place Adam in the garden He planted just for him. Things looked good but not very good—yet. The angels must have sensed that the Father was not done because the Word would be married according to the Heavenly books. If this first Adam was to be a representation of the second Adam, the Christ, where and who was his wife? We are not told in Scripture how long Adam remained single. After God gave Adam a job, he was then instructed about what and what not to eat (Genesis 2:15-17).

At some point along the way, God looked at Adam and concluded it was not good for him to be alone. Though God had created helpers for him, and all creation played a role in assisting him in fulfilling his unique assignment, the existing creation was insufficient. God knew this, but Adam had not yet recognized his need, so God, in His sovereignty, made a helper—a bride—suitable for Adam

(Genesis 2:18). Since the first Adam is a shadow of the second Adam, I believe, at some point in eternity past, God came to the same conclusion about His only begotten Son. Christ also needed a bride. Therefore, He created the Redeemed for Christ, just as He created Eve for Adam.

One would have thought that after God said He would make a suitable helper for Adam; He would have done it immediately. Instead, the Creator gave Adam a huge assignment: to name all the living creatures that God had formed out of the ground. I am looking forward to watching the video book in Heaven to see how long it took Adam to give names to all those living creatures (Genesis 2:19). Adam had a lot of pets!

Pets In Heaven

People often ask if there are animals in Heaven and if theirs will go to Heaven. There would be no animals on Earth if there were none in Heaven. The Bible tells us that Jesus is returning with armies riding on horses (Revelation 19:11, 14). Since God created the Earth to reflect Heaven and made man in His image and likeness, it is a no-brainer that He created man's earthly home with some Heavenly characteristics. The difference, of course, is that the Earth, in its original state before the fall, was merely a miniature shadow of Heaven. There is much more in Heaven than on Earth because our world was created as a temporary habitation. The Redeemed have a final, more excellent destination—the new Heaven and Earth.

Before any animal got its earthly name, it was called a living creature (Genesis 2:19). Your pet bunny, for instance, was called a living creature before receiving its earthly name, rabbit. There are countless living creatures in Heaven, and four of them serve at the Father's throne (Revelation 4:6). They all talk in a language we can understand (Revelation 5:13-14, 6:1). To answer the question of whether your pets will go to Heaven, I say yes because Heaven was made for living creatures also. God promised to liberate creation from its "bondage to decay," meaning sickness and death, and bring them into the glorious freedom of the children of God (Romans 8:20-21). When your pets die, they are freed from the curse of death and enter the glories of Heaven. Once there, they eagerly await your arrival so they can finally worship with you and carry out conversations unhindered. God is good!

A Search For A Bride

When Adam was finished giving names to the living creatures, a search was conducted for a fitting helpmate for him. How do I know this? The Bible said, "No suitable helper was found" (Genesis 2:20). For something not to have been found, a purposeful search must first be conducted. Whenever I read the Bible, as I previously told you, I like to picture what goes on behind the scenes. Indulge me momentarily and go with me on this imaginary trip. We will discover how close my imaginative ideas came to the real deal when we get to Heaven and watch the video books.

I mentally see Adam's quest for a helpmeet unfold like a story between a frustrated son and a loving father. After a fruitless search, I imagine him returning to God with downcast eyes because he came up empty, and here's how the conversation goes:

God: Son, you did a great job naming all the living creatures. We are so proud of you!

Adam: Thanks, dad.

God: It blesses me to see you exercise dominion over the Earth.

Adam: (With a sad look) Thanks, dad. I enjoyed doing it.

God: Are you okay? You don't seem so happy.

Adam: Well, (he sighs), we just finished searching for a suitable helper for me and found none.

Can You make me one?

God: Sure! But it's going to cost you something.

Adam: (His face brightens before he asks a question with an inquisitive expression) "What exactly will it cost me, Dad—some territory on the Earth?

God: Oh, much more than that, son. You'll have to lay down your life and trust me to bring you back to life."

Adam: And?

God: It will involve the breaking of your body and the shedding of your blood. Think about it, son, and let Me know.

Adam: (Remaining in deep thought for some time, then looking up to God excitedly) I'm in, Dad.

Let's do it!

The Process

According to Genesis 2:21, God caused Adam to fall into a deep sleep. In this verse, deep sleep in Hebrew translates into supernatural sleep. This word choice indicates that this was no ordinary nap. It reminds me of how a doctor uses powerful anesthesia to make sure their patient is unconscious before performing a surgical procedure. While Adam was out, his body was broken, which must have resulted in the shedding of his blood. God then took one of Adam's ribs and closed the place with flesh. Adam's body and blood paid the bride price for Eve. In the same way, Jesus' body was broken, and His blood was shed to pay the bride price for the Redeemed (Revelation 5:9-10).

In some tribes in my homeland, a portion of the bride price is given to the bride. If she receives it, it becomes a token of her willingness to take the man as her groom. Each time we receive Jesus' body and blood at the communion table, we say yes to His bride price and Him as our groom.

The Wedding

When God made a woman from Adam's rib, I visualize the angels unable to contain their excitement. Finally, all that the angels had read in the libraries of Heaven about the Lamb's wedding feast must have begun making some sense. A helper had been created for Adam. Next, they got to witness their first-ever wedding ceremony!

Preparations must have taken off in full gear.

I have no idea how much time God spent with Eve after He created her and before He walked her down the aisle. I am uncertain how much He shared with her about herself and the man who paid such a significant bride price for her. I can't say how He answered the questions that Eve, like any other bride, must have asked. Someday, the video book in Heaven will fill in the blanks.

As everyone in Heaven looked forward to the wedding of the Lamb, I don't think it was only the angels who were happy for Adam and enthusiastic about the following line of events. I believe the Father was, too. I don't know who officiated this wedding. Still, innumerable angels had to attend because the King was giving His daughter away in marriage. What a celebration Heaven's first marriage ceremony on Earth must have been. I can see Adam gazing as the Father walked his bride up to him. He must have been bubbling over with joy as he described Eve as "bone of my bone" and "flesh of my flesh" and called her woman (Genesis 2:22-23).

Just as there was no suitable helper for Adam until Eve was formed, none of the angelic beings qualified to be the bride of Christ. If they did, there would have been no need for the Redeemed. We are the only suitable helpmates for the Son of God. What an honor to be counted among the Redeemed!

The First Couple: A Type of Christ and His Bride

Adam was made from the dust of the Earth. He did not come alive until God breathed into him (Genesis 2:7). Gabriel visited Mary with the good news that she would become the mother of Jesus. Just like the first Adam, the second Adam did not come to life inside Mary's womb until the Holy Spirit rested upon her and overshadowed her (Luke 1:35). Both Adams became living beings by an act of God's breath and Spirit. Moreover, as the first bride, Eve, was made from Adam laying down his life, the bride of Christ, the Redeemed, was birthed from Jesus laying down His life.

Now the LORD God had formed out of the ground all the beasts of the field and all the birds of the air. He brought them to the man to see what he would name them, and whatever the man called each living creature, that was its name. So, the man gave names to all the livestock, the birds of the air, and all the beasts of the field. However, no suitable helper was found for Adam (Genesis 2:19-20).

I once asked the Lord why He waited until Adam had finished naming the living creatures before the search for a suitable helpmate began. I was curious because there are no insignificant details in the Bible. God could have made Eve before Adam named all the living creatures, but He did not. Thankfully, the Holy Spirit granted my request and revealed the answer. He showed me that Adam named the living creatures to exercise dominion on Earth. For the first Adam to be an appropriate symbolic representation of the second Adam, he had to rule and use his dominion before the formation of Eve. That's because Jesus Christ was already ruling and reigning before the formation of His bride. God is genuinely into the details.

A Side Note

I wonder what would happen to modern divorce rates if we all followed God's recipe for finding a wife or husband. The right man for a daughter of God, per God's Genesis recipe, must be a living soul who fears God; regularly fellowships with God; hears and speaks to God; takes his concerns to God; has a job; is walking in obedience to God; and is willing to lay down his life for his wife.

Per God's Genesis recipe, the right woman for a son of God must be a living soul who fears God, is a suitable helper, is brought to the man by God, is already walking with God, hears and speaks to God, and is willing to spend the rest of her life with her husband.

First Adam, Then Eve. Why So?

I was fascinated to discover how God painted a picture of our Redeemer through Adam and Eve and the order of their creation. For example, Adam had to be made first because Jesus is the first. He is the head of His body, the church (Colossians 1:18). In the birthing process, under normal circumstances, babies are born headfirst, followed by the body. Therefore, Adam, who is the head of the wife (Ephesians 5:23) had to be formed first, followed by his bride. Only God could have inspired the writing and assembly of what we know today as the Bible. The intentionality behind how and where things are placed in this holy book and how they came into being could only have been orchestrated by God Almighty.

The Fall

In the fall of the first couple, we see a shadow of Christ and His bride. Have you ever wondered why Satan tempted Eve and not Adam? As a foreshadowing of the Word, Adam would not have fallen into Satan's trap. Before Satan was kicked out of Heaven, he most likely spent time in the libraries of Heaven reading the book about man's creation and redemption. Somehow, Satan knew he could not take Adam out. He had to go through the weaker vessel, the woman (1 Peter 3:7). He waited until Eve was formed before launching his attack. The Bible records that it was the woman, not Adam, who was deceived and became a sinner (1 Timothy 2:14).

Adam could have walked away and left his bride in her fallen state, but he chose to die with her. In the same way, on the cross of Calvary, Jesus did not just die with His bride— represented by the sinners hanging on either side of Him (Matthew 27:38)—He also died for His bride. He chose to buy back His bride with His life. Both the first and second Adam sacrificed their lives. The difference is that the first Adam died in disobedience, while the second Adam died in obedience. To our Heavenly Father, obedience is better than sacrifice (1 Samuel 15:22-23). Jesus redeemed us by His sacrificial obedience (1 Corinthians 6:20). If Jesus had died in disobedience, we would not have been redeemed. Obedience is the key to God's heart; it is God's love language (John 14:15; 1 John 2:3-6).

Master Craftsman

I mentioned earlier that Satan possibly read a lot while still in Heaven, serving as a covering cherub (Ezekiel 28:13-15). He knew not to tempt Adam and that the weaker vessel, the woman, was the one to target. However, he did not know or forgot that God is a master craftsman. If Satan had remembered that he would have known that whatever he meant for evil, God would work it out for good (Romans 8:28-31).

When Satan succeeded in causing man to sin, resulting in our broken world, God unveiled many of His hidden attributes that had been previously unknown to man and angels. To illustrate, until Satan caused man to sin, Adam did not know God could make leather clothing.

He discovered this only after giving in to temptation (Genesis 3:21). Furthermore, before man transgressed, neither humankind nor heavenly beings had experienced God as a redeemer. Though He always was a redeemer, this side of Him was not manifested until man succumbed to temptation, creating the need for redemption.

In my relationship with God, there are attributes of the Father that I did not come to know until I walked through the valley of the shadow of death. The appreciation of the Lord as your shepherd deepens and grows exponentially in life's "valley seasons." My son, before he went to be with the Lord, was in the hospital for six months. In that period, I came to know multiple attributes of God. Before this, I was only aware of these divine characteristics by faith. Specifically, before this dark season, I only knew the Lord spiritually as a rock and fortress. Still, during that time, I got to know that side of Him experientially.

In short, thanks to the fall of our first parents, Adam and Eve, and our multiple falls after that, all creation is learning something extraordinary about God. Once we surrender to Him, He specializes in using the debris from our brokenness as construction materials to complete the work He began in our lives (Philippians 1:6).

Chapter Four

The Redeemed as God's Living Mobile Home

I read a book by Reverend Jesse Duplantis called *Heaven: Close Encounters of the God Kind*. It's an excellent book, and I recommend it to anyone desiring to learn more about Heaven. In it, he shared some of what he saw and heard when he was caught up in Heaven. When Reverend Duplantis was taken before the throne of God, he witnessed light beings. They were coming out from within the Father, loving on Him, and then going back into Him. The writer said he heard these light beings pleading with God to send them to earth, and he was told that they were "unborn babies" asking to be born.

Similarly, we were light beings before we became flesh. We lived in God before we showed up in our mother's womb. God is called the Father of the heavenly lights (James 1:17). We are those heavenly lights sent into the world to be the light of the world (Matthew 5:14). The word light (Phōs) in the referenced Scripture is different from the stars or moon (Phengos). Jesus used this specific word when describing Himself to His disciples as the "light of the world" (John 9:5; Matthew 5:14). It is a life-giving light, the exact word defined as life in John 1:4.

Therefore, God is light, and so are His children (1 John1:5, Matthew 5:14). Scriptures say He chose us in Christ before the creation of the world to be the light of the world while we are here (Ephesians 1:4). As lights, we are appointed to chase away the darkness. In Heaven, before I was conceived, God's body was my temple. On earth, as part of the Redeemed, my body is His temple (1 Corinthians 6:13-19). As a redeemed person on earth, I am God's mobile home!

We Chose to Be Born

Seeing the nature of our Heavenly Father throughout Scripture, I am convinced that no one was forced to participate in time. When the Father shared His plan with us in eternity past, just like Jesus and the prophet Isaiah, we were so excited and in love with Him that we asked to be a part of it (Isaiah 6:8; Hebrews 10:5-7). We may not have chosen our biological parents or the circumstances into which we were born and raised. Still, we did agree with God to journey through time. I have concluded because the Bible reveals that God governs based on agreements. In Amos 3:3, God says two cannot walk together unless they agree.

Having established our agreement with God's plan, one may wonder why any of God's heavenly lights would want to invade a dark, fallen world like ours voluntarily. As light beings in Him, we yearned to fulfill a greater purpose, and without participating in time, there are several privileges we would have missed out on.

As mere light beings, we could not rule and reign with Him (2 Timothy 2:12). We were not the bride of Christ (Revelation 19:7). We were not Christ's gift to the Father (Revelation 5:9-10). We were not the most expensive treasures in creation. We were not bought with a price (1 Corinthians 6:20). Finally, we were not seated with Christ in Heavenly places (Ephesians 2:6). These specific privileges and opportunities are reserved for the Redeemed. We wanted to be all that we could potentially be. For this reason, it was a joy to say yes to being born, especially knowing that God would never leave or forsake us.

The Gift of Free Will

We arrived in our mother's womb equipped with free will. Like the angels before us, we, too, will be tempted by Satan. Our triumphant return to the Father will hinge on whether we exercise our will in favor of following God or default to the enemy's side. Though the Redeemed will contend with temptation if we live on earth, we must persist in the things of God. It is essential to live a life worthy of our calling (Ephesians 4:1-3), and this can only be achieved if we choose to be led by the Holy Spirit (Romans 8:14). Every single person on earth is led either by the Spirit or by their fleshly nature—the latter being the way of Satan and the fallen world. There is no neutral position.

We cannot please God on our own. Still, thankfully, the Spirit of God, who has been here from the beginning, has worldwide coverage (Genesis 1:2). He comes alongside everyone who receives Him, works in their hearts, and creates opportunities for them to reconnect to God. When we accept Him, we give Him the legal right to put His seal of ownership on us and put His Spirit in our hearts as a deposit, guaranteeing what is to come (2 Corinthians 1:21-22).

We do not forfeit our right to choose as we move through time. Granted, free will seems risky because the enemy bombards us with numerous temptations. I even wished I did not have free will, mainly when I made wrong choices. But God knows we will miss the mark and take the wrong turn as we grow in our knowledge of Him. Yet, He allows us the freedom to choose. Despite our unavoidable mistakes, we can turn back to Him at any time once we discover we are on a destructive path.

Language Class

To stay on the right track in your walk of faith, you need to be able to communicate with God. If you want supernatural wisdom, guidance, and direction, He'll give it to you. Just ask the Holy Spirit to lead you (Luke 11:11-13). He loves requests like that and will gladly sign you up for what I like to call His "language class."

I vividly recall when the Lord once said, "You're asking to hear My voice more clearly when you should be asking Me to teach you My language, not just My voice because I am not limited to verbal communication. My language is multifaceted." That was a real eye-opener for me. I did not realize I was solely focusing on verbal communication. Since that time, I have enrolled in His divine language class. It teaches me to know His voice, whether He is speaking through a man or an animal, as in the case of Balaam and his talking donkey (Numbers 22:28-34).

When I think back on what God said to me regarding my limited focus on one specific method of communication, it sparks a childhood memory. As a girl, I learned to interpret my mom's nonverbal communication better than her spoken words. Here's the thing about my mother: she was a woman who didn't say too much, but her quietness did not equal passivity—not at all. Growing up, I was sure no other child had a mom as strict as mine. While I am thankful for the woman God chose to birth and raise me, she was challenging at times.

My mother would look at me, and it spoke volumes, most notably when we had guests or were out in public. She could easily convey messages without a single syllable like: "Get out of here!" "Don't you dare?" "Boy…are you in big trouble." "Are you out of your mind?" Those messages were loud and clear because I could read her nonverbal cues. So then, if our human language includes nonverbal communication, how much more with God?

Christian author Graham Cooke asked, "When God is committed to not telling you, how do you know where to go?" It's a mentally stimulating question that makes me think about a time in the Bible when God spoke to Abraham. He told the patriarch of faith to leave his country and people and go to a land God had already picked for him. Mind you, biblical records show the Lord did not tell Abraham whether he should go north, south, east, or west. Consequently, when Abraham set out on his journey, he had no idea where he was going or how far he had to travel to get there. God told him to go, and he obeyed (Genesis 12:1-4).

I would still be distressed, even having Abraham's story as a reference point, knowing that God brought him safely to the new country if the Lord challenged me to do what Abraham did. Based on the results of my DISC personality profile—a popular personal assessment that measures your personality and behavioral style—venturing out into the unknown would be a problem for me. My scores indicate that I am among 17 percent of the human population that likes details. People like me need clearly outlined instructions with no gray areas. Nevertheless, my personality and preferences, no matter what they are, do not dictate how God chooses to do things. He doesn't adapt His methods to suit my desires.

This year will mark 44 years of walking with God, and I can tell you that He does not tweak His language class to accommodate you. But if you let Him, the Holy Spirit will help you make all the internal adjustments necessary to communicate with God and understand His verbal and nonverbal language. The Spirit will enlarge your capacity and make up for what you lack so you can excel in that language class despite your personality.

A House to Host

I enjoy shopping for homes. I've done it four times so far in my adult life. I consider the size and layout when determining whether a house is satisfactory. Does it have enough room for a Bible study group? How many people can sit comfortably in the dining area? Things like this matter to me.

While I am not an extrovert, my husband and I must have enough space to welcome a group of people into our home. That way, if the Lord requires that of us, we can do it. I also like to host angels. One of the ways I do this is by inviting the saints in. I know that wherever they go, their angels follow! I also ensure a potential home has proper sound insulation and a room big enough for me to dance without being too disruptive to the neighbors. I can be loud when I praise and worship in my house.

Recently, the Lord began to teach me the importance of having room to host all the blessings He wants to give us. Such would not be possible if I bought a house that was too small. There would be no room to dance, thus hindering my worship at home. Without a place to host the saints, I could not fulfill my desire to host their angels. In Scripture, there are abundant promises and blessings Jesus obtained for us through His death. I want to receive them all, including the promised glory of which He speaks.

Despite my great desire, I have not yet seen the manifestation of the mind-blowing level of glory some men and women of the Old Testament experienced. But why? The Bible says we have a better covenant than Enoch, Moses, Elijah, David, and Solomon; they all died before Christ redeemed us by His death. On the other hand, we are living in a time when the work of Calvary is complete, and we have access to all those great benefits.

Yet, the depth of the glory those guys experienced appears rare in our time.

Don't get me wrong, I know that Christ in me is the hope of glory, and I know that I have the resurrected Christ in me. I have no dissatisfaction with or in God. My desire for more stems from knowing that our Heavenly Father designed the path of the Redeemed as a shining light that shines brighter and brighter until the perfect day (Proverbs 4:18). As grateful as I am for however bright my light is currently shining,

I am like a kid looking forward to another Christmas, knowing that more gifts are coming to me. The Redeemed, with unveiled faces, all reflect the Lord's glory, but there is more because wherever you are today is not the finish line. We are being transformed from glory to glory (2 Corinthians 3:18)!

I desire everything Jesus' blood purchased for me, including a measure of glory both within and upon me (Isaiah 60:1-3), because I know it is the Father's will for the Redeemed. I asked for more since Scripture says we have not because we ask not (James 4:2). But then, the Lord opened my eyes to see I was asking amiss. He said, "You ask Me for water, and I send you rain, but you have nothing to collect the water. Even with a downpour of rain, you would still have no water. The problem is not with Me. I want to bless you more than you can imagine.

My blessings have been poured out, but you do not have what is needed to host the blessings you are asking for. My blessings flow where there is room for them."

Because of that, I have changed the way I pray. I now ask the Holy Spirit to create in me whatever is missing. I also request that He remove from me anything that would hinder me from hosting the blessings for which I have prayed. I am God's habitation, as are all the Redeemed. As such, we must have enough room to host God's agenda.

A Move-In Ready House

I used to think I was a do-it-yourself person, but when I met my husband, it became apparent that my DIY skills were limited. I can read the instructions on a newly purchased item and attempt to assemble it as instructed, but that's as far as it goes. My husband, on the other hand, can fix anything. I may be bragging about him, but he's earned it. I can't remember ever calling in a plumber, carpenter, or electrician to repair anything since we got married. That's why we look for different things when we go house shopping. I hunt for a move-in ready home, and he is drawn to the fixer-uppers!

As the Redeemed, some of our blessings, breakthrough seasons, or special requests may be delayed because we are not "move-in ready." I have experienced the power of God in my life. Still, when I compare my experiences to what I read about in the Scriptures, I feel like I've only seen ripple waves instead of the promised tidal waves. One time, I talked to the Lord about this. He told me He wanted to grant my request, but if He did so, the wave would take me out. I was not move-in ready for that blessing. I prayed that the Holy Spirit would make me move in, ready for a greater measure of God's power.

Growing up with an introverted single mother, we occasionally hosted people at home. On those rare occasions when visitors came by, we used unique dishes and silverware strictly set aside for those moments. Whenever my mom asked us to bring out these items, I knew someone important was coming over. In addition, my mom would put on what she called "outfits to see the king," which were her finest clothing and jewelry items.

In the Bible, the kingdom of God is described as a large house with many vessels—some for honorable use and others for common use. If anyone cleanses themselves, Scripture says, they will be fit to be used for noble purposes (2 Timothy 2:20-21). The Redeemed of the Lord, once they are sanctified, are move-in ready and able to be used as vessels of honor.

A House for Display

Realtors will tell you that staging a house and making it look more attractive is essential to selling it. In much the same way, the Redeemed are Christ's display models. We are ambassadors on earth and are presented for the world to see and be attracted to. God does not just want to live in you; He wants His glory to rest upon you for all to witness. In Matthew 5:14, Jesus calls you "a city set on a hill." Further, He makes the point that no one lights a lamp and puts it under a bushel, but it is placed on a candlestick to give light to all in the house.

You were made to shine for the glory of God. Yet, occasionally, He will keep you hidden for a season of growth and development. This, however, is temporary. At the right time, as determined by God, in some way, you will be put on display so nations and kings will be drawn to the brightness of the light of the Redeemed (Isaiah 60:3). On the day of Pentecost, God lit up the 120-faithful people with tongues of fire that sat on each person's head (Acts 2:3).

As you can see, God likes to market His product His way and in His perfect timing. This was evident on the day of Jesus' baptism. God sent the Holy Spirit to rest on Him as a dove, which was how the Father publicly announced Jesus as His son. God did something similar when Jesus took Peter, James, and John to the mountain to pray (Matthew 17:1-8). Since then, God has not changed; He has no reason to. Life is broken up into seasons. Just as Christ did, you will have private and public ministry times.

Keep in mind that the display of the Redeemed is not always flamboyant. For example, when Jesus was hung and displayed on the cross as the Savior of the world, there was nothing attractive or glamorous about that. When Paul was serving in ministry, at one point, he felt that God had put him and his team on display in a negative way—"like those condemned to die in the arena." Once again, nothing was attractive about that (1 Corinthians 4:9).

The life of the Redeemed is a surrendered life that the Father can display however and whenever He chooses.

Chapter Five

The Redeemed as Different Types of Houses

I lived in Aberdeen, Scotland, for a few years. One of the things I liked about Aberdeen was its granite houses. Merely driving through the city and its neighborhood inspired me; those granite houses spoke to my heart. They reflected strength, longevity, and durability and were built to last. By nature, if I like something or find it helpful, I want it to last forever. I don't like good things to be temporary. I find Heaven appealing because it is a good place with perfect things that last forever. As God's temple, which is His house, like the granite houses in Aberdeen, I want to be inspirational, too.

When my husband and I met, I lived in Scotland, and he lived in the United States. After deciding to make our home in the US, I started looking at houses online in his area of residence. Before that time, I had yet to pay close attention to the materials used to build homes in different parts of the world. I remember wondering why people got so excited about granite countertops on Home & Garden Television, also known as HGTV. I thought, why would I want a granite countertop in my kitchen? My whole house at the time was built with granite.

However, I understood the fascination with granite countertops when I noticed that most of the houses in the area were constructed from wood. Initially, that was a big surprise for me. In my ignorance, I did not realize that wooden homes could last many years with good maintenance. Still, houses made of wood did not spark the same excitement in me as granite ones. I understand that everybody is diverse and likes different things. I am thankful for a God of variety who meets each person's desires.

As the Redeemed, our foundation, as well as what we are built with, matters. Christ is our foundation, and we must remain deeply rooted in Him. We do this by hearing and doing His Word.

Any infrastructure, if it stands on any ground other than the Word, is on sinking sand. It will inevitably be eroded by the inescapable storms of life that everyone, regardless of their persuasion, goes through (Matthew 7:24-27). Therefore, it is important to build other people up with the truth of God's Word; each man's work will be tested by the fire of God. The outcome of the test determines our eternal reward. I want to avoid entering Heaven bankrupt because I failed to build other people up with quality materials.

> *If any man builds on this foundation using gold, silver, costly stones, wood, hay, or straw, his work will be shown for what it is because the Day will bring it to light. It will be revealed with fire, and the fire will test the quality of each man's work. If what he has built survives, he will receive his reward. If it is burned up, he will suffer loss; he will be saved, but only as one escaping through the flames. (1 Corinthians 3:12-15)*

If I am going to build others up with gold, silver, or costly stones, I must first possess these precious metals and gems myself. Such materials are treasures that can only be mined from the Word of God and our close fellowship with Him. To obtain these materials, we must dig deep into God's Word and understand His ways and principles, which go beyond just experiencing His deeds (Psalm 103:7).

We cannot cheapen the materials, ignore God's blueprint, and expect an outcome pleasing to God. Consider these three times in Scripture when God asked

His friends to build a dwelling place: Noah's Ark, the Tabernacle, and the Temple. On each occasion, He gave them a specific design. He also detailed how to erect the dwelling place and what materials to use. In Exodus 20:40, God commanded Moses to build according to the pattern shown to him. No doubt, God is exceptionally particular when it comes to building; I believe it's one of Jesus' favorite things to do. Think about it. Out of all the professions He could have chosen while walking the earth as a man, He chose to be a carpenter!

Six Types of Houses

All humans are created as dwelling places; as the Redeemed, we are mobile homes for God. The kind of home we are is determined by who we yield our rooms to. In studying the Word, I observed six types of human mobile homes on Earth:

1) God's House, Holy Spirit's Temple

If people yield every known area of their life to Christ and actively practice being led by the Holy Spirit, they can be described as hot and on fire for God (Revelation 3:14-16). Those who fit this classification are passionate about the things of God (1 Corinthians 3:9; 1 Corinthians 6:13-19) and live solely to carry out His agenda. Jesus, during His earthly ministry, was a perfect example of a living, breathing, mobile temple of God (John 2:19-21).

When I think of biblical examples of God's houses, the following people readily come to mind: Jesus' apostles; Job, who was the most righteous man of his time (Job 1:8); Daniel, who was highly esteemed with an excellent spirit (Daniel 9:23); Mary, the mother of Jesus, who was highly favored of God (Luke 1:28); and Apostle Paul who was wholly committed to Christ (Philippians 1:21).

2) Empty House

A person who is an empty house is just that—empty. No one was designed to be vacant, and an unoccupied house can only remain that way for a very short time. Demons that were cast out of this type of person will return because the host has not put their faith in Jesus as their Savior or submitted to His headship. Therefore, unclean spirits will overtake them.

Scripture says in Matthew 12:43-45 ESV:

> *When the unclean spirit has gone out of a person, it passes through waterless places seeking rest but finds none. Then it says, 'I will return to my house from which I came.' And when it comes, it finds the house empty, swept, and put in order. Then it goes and brings with*

> *it seven other spirits eviler than itself, and they enter and dwell there, and the last state of that person is worse than the first. So also, will it be with this evil generation.*

For an empty house to be a temple of God, the person must invite Jesus to inhabit them as Savior and Lord. Mary Magdalene is a good example. She was delivered from demonic possession, and she yielded her house to Christ to be occupied by the Word and His Spirit. She went on to become the first person to see the resurrected Christ. Mary also announced His resurrection and told the disciples where to meet Him (John 20:10-18).

Suppose a deserted house does not yield to the Word and His Spirit, as we already established. In that case, that person gets reoccupied by the demon that was driven out. Even more come. For this reason, it is better to cast demons out of people who desire to get rid of their demons, not the ones who like their demons. People who don't mind the occupation of evil spirits typically won't run to the Word after their deliverance. I have met individuals who liked their demons because the demons made them feel unique and different. Unfortunately, there are no friendly evil spirits. All forces of darkness are full of deceit, and they have an agenda to steal, kill, and destroy.

Understand that we are all unique and special because God created us that way. Discover your identity in Him and not in demonic manifestation. If demons can have no place in Heaven, they should have no place in you. You should not put up with anything contrary to God's agenda for your life.

3) The Halfway House

A halfway house represents a person who may have put their faith in Jesus to save them but has not yielded all areas of their life to His headship. He is the Savior of their spirit, but He is not yet Lord of their soul and body.

The halfway house is new to the kingdom of God and young in the things of the Lord. Most of the time, they have plenty of zeal without enough knowledge. They are like babies; they are immature, and their life may appear messy as they try to figure out their relationship with God. But with good instructors and a willingness to obey the Word, they can go on to be consecrated houses that are cleansed and ready to be used by the Master for honorable purposes. Scripture shows that God is protective over this group of people. Jesus warned that anyone attempting to lead these little ones astray is better off having a millstone tied around their neck and drowned in the depths of the sea (Matthew 18:6).

I was a halfway house from my teenage years throughout my early twenties. I had a lot of zeal without knowledge and had not yielded areas of my life to God. I genuinely didn't realize He expected total submission from me. I understood and mastered church traditions more than I comprehended the Word of God, so I was serving Him with many strings attached and didn't know it. I wanted the baptism of the Holy Spirit on my terms (I obviously did not get it until I was ready to receive it on His terms). I asked God for any gift but tongues. Halfway houses, as I used to be, don't intentionally hold back from God. They just don't know much about their new life in Christ. However, they willingly yield once they discover what is required of them.

4) The Lukewarm House

Lukewarm means you are neither hot nor cold. This categorization also suits you if you were once hot and have since cooled off. Lukewarm houses are middle-of-the-road believers that commonly refer to "hot" Christians as fanatics. They are focused on what is temporal and not eternal. They live for themselves, are preoccupied with the here and now, and are fixated on what is in the seen realm. They do not like to sacrifice their pleasure or be inconvenienced. They know about the Lord, but they don't know Him. Most of them think they are okay and have no need for anything.

They are blind but convinced they can see. They are naked but believe they are covered. They are poor but persuaded that they are rich (Rev 3:14-18). Jesus instructs lukewarm houses to come to Him, amend their ways, and obtain all He secured for them through redemption. What stops them from doing so is their desire to maintain their citizenship in both the kingdom of the world and the kingdom of Heaven. But this is not possible; the kingdom of Heaven does not allow dual citizenship. Thus, lukewarm houses are in danger of being rejected by the Lord (Revelation 3:16).

5) Desecrated House

Generally, desecrated houses pick and choose how far they want to go with God and what parts of the Bible they wish to obey. They allow idols in their lives and tend to adjust the Word to fit their lifestyle instead of changing their lifestyle to accommodate the Word. To clarify, an idol is any person, place, or thing that we prioritize above God, which could include ourselves or our families. In its very basic form, idolatry is turning one's heart away from God and setting it upon something else. By divine design, the heart is always fixed upon something. Still, if that something is not God, it is an idol (Ezekiel 14:5). Individuals classified as desecrated houses are not fazed by sin or uncleanness. Previously, they were consecrated, but they are now defiled.

To demonstrate, this type of person may be in church, yet practicing witchcraft; in church, yet indulging in sexual immorality, justifying their actions, and serving God with their own agenda; in church, yet a drunk, refusing to get help; in church, yet a gambler, unwilling to stop. They know the truth, shun it, and embrace lies instead. They have what Scripture calls "a form of godliness," but they deny its power.

The Bible admonishes the Redeemed to have nothing to do with this group of people.

> *But mark this: There will be terrible times in the last days. People will be lovers of themselves, lovers of money, boastful, proud, abusive, disobedient to their parents, ungrateful, unholy, without love, unforgiving, slanderous, without self-control, brutal, not lovers of the good, treacherous, rash, conceited, lovers of pleasure rather than lovers of God-- having a form of godliness but denying its power. Have nothing to do with them. (2 Timothy 3:1-5)*

> *But now I am writing you that you must not associate with anyone who calls himself a brother but is sexually immoral or greedy, an idolater or a slanderer, a drunkard or a*

swindler. With such a man do not even eat. (1 Corinthians 5:11)

Of the six different houses, we see through the Scriptures that the desecrated house irks God the most. In the time of the prophets, the nation of Israel was a desecrated house. Read through all the biblical books of the prophets, and you will see how the Israelites angered God by defiling themselves with idols. Another New Testament example is Judas, one of Jesus' twelve disciples, who was an unrepentant thief (John 12:6). God is jealous and holy and wants no other gods to take His place. Therefore, desecrated temples incur the wrath and judgment of God for their open defilement. God calls the Redeemed to be holy, for when a house is desecrated, the glory of God departs from it (Ezekiel 10:1819).

6) House of Devils

In Luke 8:26-39, a man housing about 6,000 demons was set free by Jesus Christ. The fact that thousands of evil spirits could live in a single person reveals the multi-dimensional nature of every human being. There are more realms within us than we realize, and there is more to us than the reflection we see in the mirror. Since we were designed to host the Creator, this is not surprising. It just shows you that we are larger inwardly than seen outwardly.

Jesus said, in His Father's house, there are many places of abode (John 14:2). Since we are God's house on earth, it means that, in us, there are many dwelling places or realms—enough to accommodate 6,000 demons as shown by this demoniac in Scripture. Before Mary Magdalene was set free by Jesus, she was home to seven demons (Mark 16:9). As is clearly seen, devils reside inside unredeemed people.

Chapter Six

The Redeemed as Authorized Agents to Cast Out Demons

Demons are Satan's offspring (Genesis 3:15; 6:2, Matthew 13:36-39). They are homeless, evil spirits waiting to be relocated to the lake of fire (Matthew 13:40-42, 25:41). In the meantime, they can roam the earth freely. It is the will of God for the Redeemed to keep them homeless (Mark 16:17). It appears that part of their divine punishment is the loss of their bodies. Hence, they seek bodies, preferably humans, to call home.

According to Scripture, demons can live in the bodies of fallen angels (Rev 16:13, 14). In the case of the demoniac, these evil spirits pleaded with Jesus to let them go into the pigs rather than being homeless. Again, they need a body to function. For example, a demon of lust needs a body through which to lust; a demon of anger needs a body to express itself; and a demon of gluttony needs a mouth through which to eat.

Humans are higher beings than animals. This is perfectly demonstrated in the Bible when a drove of pigs could not handle the number of demons that resided in one man. The Bible says the swine drowned after the demons switched their residence from the man's body to theirs. Unfortunately, there are many demoniacs on earth today, and the Redeemed are commanded and authorized by Jesus to drive them out (Mark 16:15-18).

Jesus gave the Redeemed authority over ALL the enemy's powers (Luke 10:19).

Hosea 4:6

In the above Bible passage, God revealed the cause of the destruction of His people; He said it was a lack of knowledge. We are told in Ephesians 6:10-13 to be strong in the Lord and His mighty power and dress in the whole armor of God. That way, we can stand against the devil's schemes because our struggle is against unseen beings.

We are a nation at war, and the majority of our casualties stem from our ignorance of who God is, who we are in Him, who our opponents are, and what their strategies entail. To be victorious, we must know three things: the tactics of our enemies, what empowers them, and what weakens them.

Can Demons Reside in a Believer?

Judas Iscariot was an apostle, yet Satan entered him and used him to betray his master, Jesus (Luke 22:3). Peter was an apostle. Yet, he was a mouthpiece for Satan when he tried to dissuade Jesus from dying on the cross (Matthew 16:23). Jesus described the woman He set free from the spirit of infirmity as a daughter of Abraham. This indicated that she was a woman of faith like her ancestor Abraham, yet she was bound for 18 years by Satan (Luke 13:10-16). Adam and Eve were holy and lived in the glory of God, yet Satan hung out with them, waiting for an unguarded moment to strike. When the opportunity arose, he struck, and the rest is history.

The Bible tells the Redeemed to guard their hearts with all diligence, for everything a person does flows from the heart (Proverbs 4:23). Jesus warned us that it is not what goes into a man's stomach that defiles him, but what comes from the heart through the mouth defiles him (Matthew 15:11; 15-20).

Believers can give Satan and his demons temporary or permanent residency within themselves. This is possible because our free will does not get revoked after we are born again.

The Holy Spirit, who inhabits our temple when we become believers, places His seal upon us, guaranteeing the fulfillment of His promises regarding what is to come. But He is not imprisoned or trapped in us. If He must leave, He can. He left Samson for a season (Judges 16:20). When the Holy Spirit left King Saul, an evil spirit was sent to take His place (1 Samuel 16:14).

In short, until their last breath, a person can accept or reject the Lord, Satan, and his demons. To be clear, there won't be people spending eternity with God who did not choose Him. By default, a person chooses Satan if they reject God.

Even so, demons know they will unlikely get a permanent camping spot in a believer's soul or flesh. Here's why: if a believer continues in the light, the demon will have no hiding place at some point. As the light of the Word permeates every fiber of the Christian's being, their mind is renewed, and their soul is transformed and conformed to the likeness of Jesus Christ. True disciples will do whatever it takes to evict a demon once they realize it has lingered inside. Therefore, demons like to keep their presence hidden or very subtle when possible. They know they will lose their accommodations if their host becomes aware of their presence and destructive activities.

What Gives Demons Rights to Afflict People?

A) God

There are protocols and rules of engagement both in the kingdom of Heaven and the kingdom of darkness. On occasion, God will permit Satan to attack a righteous person. This is what happened in the life of the apostle Paul as described in 2 Corinthians 12:6-9 ESV:

> *Though if I should wish to boast, I would not be a fool, for I would be speaking the truth. But I refrain from it, so that no one may think more of me than he sees in me or hears from me. So, to keep me from being too elated by the surpassing greatness of the revelations, a thorn was given me in the flesh, a messenger of Satan to harass me, to keep me from being too elated. Three times I pleaded with the Lord about this, that it should leave me. But he said to me, "My grace is sufficient for you, for my power is made perfect in weakness." Therefore, I will boast all the more gladly of my weaknesses, so that the power of Christ may rest upon me.*

If you recall, Satan was kicked out of Heaven due to pride. To ensure that a righteous person will not be trapped by this same sin, God permits a messenger of Satan to buffet the individual just as He did in Paul's case. Such demonic attacks, as unpleasant as they are, are divinely permitted, protective measures to keep that person humble and relatable to the souls they are called to reach.

Though God allowed the demonic assault on Paul, He also set boundaries for how far this messenger of Satan could go. This evil spirit was not given free reign and could not impact anything beyond Paul's flesh. The apostle's spirit and soul were off limits to this tormentor. Additionally, we see the same rule in operation when God lets Satan afflict Job.

> *"Skin for skin!" Satan replied. "A man will give all he has for his own life. But stretch out your hand and strike his flesh and bones, and he will surely curse you to your face." The LORD said to Satan, "Very well, then, he is in your hands; but you must spare his life." So, Satan went out from the presence of the LORD and afflicted Job with painful sores from the soles of his feet to the top of his head. (Job 2:4-7)*

When I read about these occurrences in Scripture, I am reminded that God's ways are not ours, and His thoughts are far higher than ours (Isaiah 55:8-9). For this reason, I am at peace with whatever strategy He employs for our safety and promotion, knowing full well that anything He does or allows is love-driven. He can be trusted. Though we do not know how long that messenger of Satan was allowed to harass Paul or how long Satan himself tormented Job, we do know they both won in the end.

To this day, they each stand as an example of God's power and faithfulness.

The next logical question is, how does a person know if the demonic affliction in their flesh is an attack approved by God? Doing a sin check is an excellent place to start. Ask yourself, am I living a sanctified life?

Neither Paul nor Job were practicing sin when they were assailed. In fact, God declared that Job was the most righteous person on earth in his day. Likewise, Paul was completely sold out to God during his painful experience. Both cried out to the Lord and in response, He told these holy men that their suffering was divinely permitted. Unless God tells you it's Him, then it's not. Proceed to cast that devil out.

B) Open Doors

Sin and righteousness stand at the door of our hearts, seeking entrance. Jesus stated in Revelation 3:20 that He stands at the door knocking, and whoever opens to Him will come in and dine with the person. On the other hand, if that individual does not allow Christ in, sin will permeate. Take Cain, for example. When he killed his brother, Abel, God warned him that sin was crouching at his door.

> *Then the LORD said to Cain, "Why are you angry? Why is your face downcast? If you do what is right, will you not be accepted? But if you do not do what is right, sin is crouching at your door; it desires to have you, but you must master it." (Genesis 4:6-7)*

What kinds of things can open the door to demonic affliction? Here are some: unforgiveness, personal sin, unremitted sin, generational sins, curses, demonic covenants, and possession of occult items.

The Enemy Lays Low

I recall a prophetic dream I had. In it, I encountered one of the rulers of the dark world who was laying claim to me. She told me I was dedicated to her at birth; therefore, she had a right over my life. I was enraged by that information. At the time, I had been a believer for about 23 years. In my dream, with a wave of her hand, I saw my life play like a movie. There were scenes from when I first gave my heart to the Lord at five years old and moments from the present. As I watched, she mentioned that she had been receiving reports about my church attendance and had instructed her messengers to lay low. They were not supposed to draw any attention to their presence or activities.

She thought my "church thing" was a phase and would only last a little while, but I had continued pressing into the light, and that made her mad. During this dream, I was mad, too. I was so upset I yelled back at her, telling her she had no right over my life! I grew even angrier as I saw the impact of her activities on my whole family. I demanded that the covenant be broken, but she refused. Those standing with her asked me to pay a ransom for my freedom, to which I responded, "No ransom will be paid."

Again, I insisted that this covenant be annulled based on my free will. I wanted no part of this evil pact. Some other things also happened while I was having this prophetic dream. Still, during that specific encounter, I lifted my eyes to Heaven, and there appeared to be an open portal over me. I cried out to the Lord and started speaking in tongues while gazing into Heaven. My Heavenly Father responded, and I came out victoriously.

Growing in the light, moving away from the peripheral, and delving deep into the Word was a game-changer for me. I did have a few other experiences with those spirit beings. Still, it was evident during future interactions that I was firmly rooted in Christ and belonged to Him.

I shared this story to let you know that, sometimes, the enemy lays low for a season, hoping not to be discovered. Demonic forces wait for the chance to strike their victims. In my case, I did not know I was dedicated to this being at birth. I'm not even sure who in my bloodline entered this demonic covenant on my behalf. Still, that wicked alliance had given demons legal rights over certain areas of my life.

Rules of Engagement

If Satan or his demons are legally camping in a place, you cannot bind and cast them out. Think about it this way: naturally, you cannot arrest someone who is not trespassing. In the same way, in the spirit realm, demons must first be made illegal before you can remove them. Jesus said that to plunder a strongman's house, you must first bind him (Mark 3:27). By calling it "a strongman's house," Jesus was letting us know that the strongman was a legal resident in that place.

The account of the paralytic who was brought to Jesus illustrates this story. This man was afflicted by sin. Jesus first removed the man's sins, thus making the affliction illegal. Afterwards, Jesus spoke healing, and the man was restored.

> *And when he saw their faith, he said unto him, Man, thy sins are forgiven thee. And the scribes and the Pharisees began to reason, saying, Who is this which speaketh blasphemies? Who can forgive sins, but God alone? But when Jesus perceived their thoughts, he answering said unto them, What reason ye in your hearts? Whether is easier, to say, Thy sins be forgiven thee; or to say, Rise up and walk? But that ye may know that the Son of man hath power upon earth to forgive sins, (he said unto the sick of the palsy,) I say unto thee, Arise, and take up thy couch, and go into thine house. And immediately he rose up before them, and took up that whereon he lay, and departed to his own house, glorifying God. (Luke 5:20-25 KJV)*

In my situation, a demonic covenant was entered on my behalf. After I came of age and chose Jesus as my Lord and Savior, I then had a right to exercise my free will. Despite accepting Christ over 20 years earlier, that did not automatically annul the diabolical agreement. I don't know what the terms were, but the covenant remained in effect until, by the mercies of God, I was made aware of its existence. Once I knew it, I exercised my free will to be released, and I was backed up by Heaven.

If I had tried to break this covenant with my own will, choice, and power without Heaven backing me up, I would not have won. The enemy is a sore loser and cannot easily free his captives. Anyone seeking to get out of his grip must have a superior power within them. There is only one such superior power, and His name— the only name by which we can receive victory— is Jesus Christ.

In summary, covenants are legal affairs, and legal matters can only be handled by following proper legal protocols. The Bible contains instructions on how to make the enemy illegal, depending on the case, which I will discuss further in subsequent chapters.

Guard Your Heart With All Diligence, and Stay Vigilant

God revealed to Peter that Jesus was not only a prophet, but He was also the Son of God (Matthew 16:17). Peter was the one who reminded Jesus that he and the disciples had left everything to follow Him (Matthew 19:27). When Jesus was deserted by many of His followers after telling them to eat His body and drink His blood (John 6:53, 60, 66), Peter didn't follow suit. Jesus turned to the twelve and asked them if they would leave, too, and Peter boldly declared his faith in the Lord Jesus Christ.

> *"You do not want to leave, too, do you?" Jesus asked the Twelve. Simon Peter answered him, "Lord, to whom shall we go? You have the words of eternal life. We believe and know that you are the Holy One of God." (John 6:67-69)*

This same Peter, a passionate follower of Jesus Christ who received revelation from Heaven, was still susceptible to Satan. The Bible shows us that Satan slipped into Peter's body and used his mouth to rebuke Jesus for agreeing to suffer and be killed. He then began to teach them that the Son of Man must suffer many things and be rejected by the elders, chief priests, and teachers of the law, and that he must be killed and after three days rise again. He spoke plainly about this, and Peter took him aside and began to rebuke him. But when Jesus turned and looked at his disciples, he rebuked Peter. "Get behind me, Satan!" he said. "You do not have in mind the things of God, but the things of men." (Mark 8:31-33).

This Bible account shows how believers can be vulnerable to satanic infiltration. It does not matter how long you have been a Christian or what spiritual gifts you possess. If you don't stay vigilant and diligently guard your heart, you, too, can have a "Peter moment." Worse yet, you could wind up having a Judas experience; tragically, he did not recover from hosting Satan (Luke 22:3). The Bible says, if the hedge is broken, the serpent will bite (Ecclesiastes 10:8). To put it another way, if you open the door, the enemy will come in because he always takes advantage of an open door.

It makes sense that Peter later wrote to the Redeemed, warning them to be sober, self-controlled, and vigilant because the adversary, the devil, roams the earth, seeking someone to devour (1Peter 5:8). Peter was undoubtedly speaking from experience he knew the number of times he fell prey to the enemy. Hence, the need for discernment and vigilance on the part of the Redeemed cannot be overemphasized. Homeless evil spirits are Satan's foot soldiers, and like homeless people, these spirits will camp anywhere they can. They are not necessarily trapped inside a person's body either; they can go in and out to do other business and return home to their host.

Typically, demons won't leave a place without a law enforcement officer kicking them out. Believers are God's appointed law enforcement officers authorized by Heaven to expel demons (Mark 16:17). If believers don't act, these beings will remain. Jesus took immediate action and cast that devil out of Peter. Once you discern demonic activity, follow Christ's example, and do the same.

Exercise of Rights

When I became a US citizen, I was given the right to vote. That year, there was a general election, including a presidential election. For personal reasons, I exercised my right to vote in all elections except for the presidential election. Here's the point: having power, authority, or a right to do something is different from exercising that power, authority, or right.

When a person receives and believes in the Word, they are granted the right to become a child of God (John 1:12). Nevertheless, today, many people are in oppressive, depressive, or suppressive situations because they have failed to exercise their rights. Many have come to God and have been granted certain privileges as one of God's children, but they have failed to use those privileges.

When Jesus went to the temple and drove out the traders that had turned the house of God into a den of robbers, He was exercising His right as the Son of God (Jeremiah 7:11; Matthew 21:13). In the same way, we ought to walk in our dominion as children of God and drive out every unclean being. In our ignorance or rebellion days, evil spirits made their home in our bodies. But now, because our temple is God's house, the demons are trespassing, and we can expel them.

You should know that demons only assume you want them gone once you exert your authority to kick them out. If Jesus had not used His power in the temple, that place would have remained a den of robbers despite His presence. Demons are robbers that come to steal, kill, and destroy. They must be driven out; otherwise, they will stay and continue to carry on their destructive work within their host. There is a reason God gave us a "right" to become His children. It is an indication that you have a part to play in the process of becoming a child of God. Your part is exercising the rights granted to you.

If you enroll in a new health plan, any treatment you previously received or any diagnosis you were given before getting that insurance coverage is classified as a "pre-existing condition." Spiritually speaking, before coming to Christ, you had some pre-existing conditions. There were specific ways of thinking and patterns of behavior that gave demons a legal right to dwell within you. Upon receiving and believing the Word and becoming a part of the Redeemed, you were empowered by the power of the Holy Spirit to deal with those pre-existing conditions. You can now cast out demons living within you or have another believer cast them out if you are unsure how to do it (Mark 16:17).

Some Leave Right Away

Demons have different personalities. Some demonic spirits will leave a person as soon as that person gives their life to Christ because they do not want to deal with even a flicker of light. Conversely, some stay put, hoping the person does not exercise their right to evict them. There are demons you can cast out by a simple command in the name of Jesus, and others you can only dislodge by prayer and fasting (Matthew 17:21 KJV).

Demons know if you legitimately belong to Christ and how much authority you command (Acts 19:11-20). The Redeemed are a part of God's army; all armies have officers of different ranks. Demons know your rank, your corresponding authority, and if you are living right before God. This is no secret in the realm of the spirit.

Many years ago, I was part of a deliverance team. We had prayed for many people and driven out demons from them. All was going well until we came to one lady. Like Jesus' disciples, we had a difficult time trying to expel the evil spirit from this woman (Mark 9:17-29). In need of reinforcement, our team leader sent for our Bishop, who was in his office at the time as soon as he stepped into the sanctuary, before getting to the lady who was lying on the floor or even saying a word, the evil spirit left.

Seeing that happen was like taking a Spiritual Authority 101 class. It taught me that we don't all command the same authority in the realm of the spirit because we are all at different levels of spiritual maturity. Authority usually goes with responsibility. The more responsibility the Father gives you, the more authority you will be entrusted with to complete your task.

I want to add that when our team had difficulty casting the demon out of the woman, our inability did not indicate a lack of prayer, fasting, or faith. We had all those areas covered, and as I said before, we had already cast out several demons in that meeting. Because the Bishop was a higher-ranking officer of God, when he arrived on the scene, the spirit left immediately.

There's an excellent Bible story that serves as a great reference point for this principle. In the book of Daniel, we are told of an angel who left Heaven to bring answers to Daniel's prayer. But the angel was met with resistance from a spiritual entity, a fallen angel of the kingdom of darkness. For 21 days, the angel was detained until Michael, a higher-ranking officer of God and a chief commander of Heaven's armies, showed up (Daniel 10:10-14). After Michael's arrival, the delay ended.

Divine Protocols

Recently, while seeking deliverance for a brother in the Lord, our team came up against a defiant demon. We asked the demon why it would not leave. This evil spirit told us two things: one, when it had come in, and two, who opened the door for it to have a legal right to this brother's flesh. After gaining that insight, we confessed the sins, brought repentance over the matters raised, and put them under the blood of Jesus. Next, the demon stated that there was one last protocol we missed, and until that protocol was followed, it had a right to stay. I asked it, what protocol? It said it would not tell me, and why would it?

A few days later, the Lord revealed what the issue was. It turned out an occult object was in the house. A rug with demonic images had been purchased at a Goodwill store, and no one had previously noticed. As soon as this was revealed, we rolled up the rug and removed it from the house. Once we took that item outside, the brother said he felt instantly better.

Demonic or occult objects—things devoted to evil spirits—can give the enemy a right to remain and operate in a place. Be careful. Go through your stuff prayerfully. Identify and remove accursed objects from your environment (Joshua 6:18). In the Bible, the Israelite army, under the leadership of Joshua, was defeated by an insignificant army because they violated divine protocol. A man named Achan kept certain items the Lord had instructed the Israelites to destroy. Many died due to the accursed things in his possession (Joshua 7:10-12; 20-21).

My Deliverance Story

I put my faith in Jesus as my Lord and Savior when I was five. I did not know much about deliverance or demonic activity until I was in my early twenties. Having been given knowledge and understanding, I received prayer from my youth group. I did not know if I had any demons residing within me, but I chose to present myself for a checkup.

Sure enough, when the team prayed over me, they saw beings leaving. One of the demons that exited was a religious spirit. The prayer team knew how to classify this being because it was decked with religious artifacts. I was not surprised by that at all; I was very religious for several years before that day. When they were finished praying, I felt like I had just taken a thorough bath. I can't explain it, but I sensed I was clean. It seemed like a heavy weight had been lifted.

Before my deliverance, I used to have what I would call unclean and defiling dreams. In my sleep, evil spirits would come with familiar faces to defile me, and I could do nothing about them. All that changed following my supernatural release. I could fight and refuse to be defiled when those beings showed up. It felt so good waking up in victory. As I immersed myself more in the Word of God, I began living out biblical principles and allowed the Word to dwell in me. The corrupting dreams stopped altogether. I am thankful God made a way for us to be clean and stay clean. The Word truly is a cleansing agent.

I have driven out demons from believers before, and this should not be viewed as shameful. Satan would love for people to be too embarrassed to go for a checkup. Do not let him fool you. You may need a personal soul checkup if you can't grow beyond where you were when you first believed in Christ, are experiencing recurring defiling dreams, are suffering from chronic ailments, can't seem to receive the baptism of the Holy Spirit, have problems retaining Scripture; have sinful habits you can't break; have issues reading the Bible and praying; fall asleep every time the Word is being preached.

If you recognize disturbing patterns in your life, don't be too ashamed to do a checkup. You have nothing to lose. The worst that can happen is you'll get prayed for and leave with a blessing.

Why Drive Out Demons

All demons share the same agenda as Satan: they come to steal, kill, and destroy. It does not matter how harmless they pretend to be; their goal is to hinder a person from being all God created them to be and destroy their destiny. Until the time comes for demons to be hurled into the lake of fire with Satan, our Job is to keep them homeless.

The authority to drive out demons is one of the privileges New Testament believers have that Old Testament saints did not. It was a distinguishing factor between the ministry of Jesus and any other prophet before Him in history (Matthew 9:33). As the Redeemed, we must use every strategy provided by God, our commander in chief, to win battles as we journey through time. Demons are like Satan's foot soldiers in the earthly realm. Keeping them unhoused hinders satanic activities because many of them need a body through which to function. Not allowing them to reside inside us is a warfare strategy.

According to Jesus, after a demon is cast out, it goes to dry places seeking rest (Luke 11:24-25). A dry place could be another person's body; I now understand why Jesus said rivers of living water will flow out of the belly of the Redeemed (John 4:14, 7:38). If you have a river flowing within you, you will never be a dry place. The dry place is the wandering arena of demons. Don't be a dry place.

I cannot overstress that the Redeemed must not be afraid of demons. All power in Heaven and earth belongs to Jesus Christ, who is the One who commissioned us to drive out demons in the first place (Matthew 28:18). Jesus also gave us authority over ALL the powers of the enemy (Luke 10:19 KJV). If you encounter demonic beings that resist you, call for reinforcement.

For a moment, imagine one police officer showing up where people experiencing homelessness are unauthorized to be and asking them to leave. Some will likely be defiant because there is only one officer, right? Now, imagine the policeman calling for backup. When a crew of policemen arrives, even the most rebellious ones will vacate the premises. The resisters may successfully overpower one officer, but they know they cannot overpower a troop.

This principle applies in the kingdom of God (Leviticus 26:8). The Bible says, one of us may put a thousand to flight. Still, two will put ten thousand to flight (Deuteronomy 32:30 -31). When confronted with a stubborn demonic spirit, get one or more other believers to stand with you because there is power in numbers. Moreover, Jesus promised that whenever two or three are gathered in His name, He is there in their midst

(Matthew 18:20). You cannot lose with Jesus on your side. Just remember, it is a battle and not a dance party. You will face resistance, so take your stand as an armed soldier dressed for war. Put on the complete armor of God (2 Corinthians 10:4-5; Ephesians 6:11). Be ready in and out of season.

Chapter Seven

The Redeemed Process of Becoming a Residence for the Godhead

When we receive Christ, God deposits His Spirit in us as a guarantee of what is to come (Ephesians 1:13-14). A deposit indicates that there is more available to you. You don't automatically receive all you are entitled to in the kingdom of God. Becoming a son of God involves a process with no shortcuts.

To explain, we all start as infants and grow into mature sons (Galatians 4:1-3). However, it is common to find babes in Christ who assume they are mature based on their age, gift, or knowledge. Maturity does not come with natural age, gifting, or educational qualifications. On the contrary, it results from feasting on the Word of God, submitting to it, and applying it to every area of your life. Maturity results from picking up your cross daily and being a faithful disciple of Christ (John 8:31).

When you obey the Word, the Godhead—the Father, Son, and Holy Spirit—you make your body their abode. When the Godhead lives in you, you no longer have just a deposit of the Spirit, but the Father and Son join the Holy Spirit, and they all dwell in you as one (John 14:23). At this point, no demon can reside in you. Some demonic spirits will flee as soon as you show up in a place, and those that are living inside other people may start manifesting when you are present (Mark 1:21-28). This is the inheritance of the Redeemed (John 17:20-23). This was the level Jesus operated on when He walked the earth. The fullness of the Godhead dwelled in bodily form in Christ, the Son of Man, as an example to us, the Redeemed (Colossians 2:9).

How to Maintain Our Bodies as a Dwelling Place of the Godhead

Flee Sexual Immorality

Jesus commanded us to be wise as serpents and gentle as doves. Ecclesiastes 3:1 teaches us that there are times and seasons for every activity under Heaven. There is even a time to stand flat-footed and resist the devil and a time to simply flee. Believers are advised in Scripture to flee, meaning run, from sexual immorality (1 Corinthians 6:18).

In Genesis 39:12, Joseph fled from Potiphar's wife when she attempted to lure him into sexual sin. He paid a price for his integrity, but God honored him, and he went from the prison to the palace. On the other hand, many have corrupted their houses by trying with all their might to resist the devil when they should have been fleeing. Obey the Bible's command to run away from sexual immorality, and don't allow the enemy to get a foothold in this area. Otherwise, he will build a stronghold. To keep our bodies holy, we must run to escape immorality in all its shades and forms.

Seek First the Kingdom of God

If we first seek the kingdom of God and His righteousness in all our pursuits, defilers hoping to taint our bodily temple won't enjoy hanging around. We will not be considered good company.

Intimate Relationship With the Word

- How do you reclaim the devil's house? The Word.
- How do you fill an empty house? The Word.
- How do you cleanse a desecrated house? The Word.

The difference between a house of God and the other kinds of houses can be traced to each person's relationship with the Word. Communion with Christ and a strong desire to obey Him will always produce a dwelling place for the Godhead. Draw near to God, and He will draw near to you (James 4:8). <u>Stay rooted in the Word</u>, abide in Him, and allow His words to abide in you. Look daily in the mirror of the Word of God and be sure not to use it just as a rear-view mirror, or you will only see others and rarely see yourself. You will not be impacted by what you read, and your spiritual growth will be prolonged or come to a complete halt. Those who meditate on Scripture and apply it are usually quick to repent. Bible application and swift repentance are the ways they stay clean.

Obedience

We are commanded to both hear and obey the Word. This is made easier through intimacy with Christ because it attunes our ears to His voice. Learning to listen and obey is critical since our love for God is measured by our obedience to Him. Jesus said that those who love Him obey Him (John 14:15). The Bible tells us that during the days of Jesus' earthly life, His prayers were answered because of His deep reverence for God (Hebrews 5:7). That Word reverent, which means to show deep and solemn respect, seems to be missing in our western culture. It is also greatly lacking in Pentecostal and Charismatic denominations—though this is not true of all believers in these circles. Yet, reverent is a word that describes the culture of Heaven.

Thankfully, during my years in Catholic school, I was well-prepared to walk reverentially before the Lord. My schoolmates and I were taught reverential fear and worshipful awe of God in middle and high school. We were instructed on how to behave, especially in the sanctuary or any place set aside for corporate worship. It's a good thing that, still today, there are cultures in the world that promote honor and respect for the Lord, as God never leaves Himself without a witness. I believe Christian parents owe it to their children to teach them to be pious and devout disciples of Jesus.

Perhaps our lack of reverential worship has something to do with our unanswered prayers. God is to be revered if you want your prayers to be unhindered. We must never get so familiar with Him that we forget that He is God Almighty.

Different Types of Obedience

There are various types of obedience: regular, sacrificial, complete, and incomplete. Each type attracts different responses from God.

Regular Obedience

Regular obedience does not call for any sacrifice because what is being asked of us does not disrupt our comfort and falls in line with our strengths or delights. For example, James 1:19 says we should be quick to listen, slow to speak, and slow to become angry. For someone with an introverted personality, obeying this Scripture might not be as difficult as it would be for an extrovert. Introverts are naturally quieter and more reserved. They prefer to keep their opinions to themselves and remain in the background. Contrastingly, extroverts tend to be more outspoken and vocal, so they need to work harder to obey this command.

Sacrificial Obedience

Any directive from God that stretches you beyond the limits of your comfort zone requires sacrificial obedience. If you want to see a perfect model of this kind of obedience, look no further than Abraham, who offered up his son Isaac to God (Genesis 22:1-19). Hebrews 5:8 says Jesus "learned obedience through what He suffered." For a long time, that passage did not make sense to me. How could Jesus learn obedience? Was He not always obedient? Was He not an obedient son before He embarked on His journey through time as a man?

To answer my question, the Spirit of God revealed the various types of obedience. He taught me that Jesus was indeed always obedient to the Father. Still, Christ's obedience was not sacrificial before His journey to earth. It was normal, birthed from a place of strength and delight. When Jesus obeyed the Father by being made flesh and dwelling among men, this was a completely new experience for Him. Moreover, giving His life for man's redemption was the greatest sacrifice ever offered through all of time and eternity. Jesus' sacrificial obedience began from the moment He was made flesh until He hung on Calvary's tree.

When the Word Chose to Comply

- Jesus, as God, chose to fit into human flesh and allowed Himself to be restrained to one earthly location at a time was sacrificial.
- Jesus, as God, allowing Himself to eat food from a fallen world, was sacrificial.
- Jesus, as God, was sacrificial by allowing Himself to walk on dusty roads instead of streets paved with gold and by traveling in a boat instead of riding on the wings of cherubs.
- Jesus as God, allowing Himself to experience exhaustion as a human, consequently needing sleep, was sacrificial (Luke 8:23-30).

- Jesus, as God, restraining Himself from commanding the angels to destroy His crucifiers, was sacrificial (Matthew 26:53).
- To crown it all, Jesus as God, being separated from the Father through death so that He might taste death for everyone else, remains the greatest sacrifice in the history of creation (Hebrews 2:9). Jesus indeed learned sacrificial obedience through what He suffered.

The excellent news about sacrificial obedience is that it carries a weightier reward than regular obedience, so don't miss any opportunity to be sacrificially obedient to God. Jesus was rewarded for His sacrificial obedience by being given a name above all names (Philippians 2:9). God is drawn to sacrifice. We see it from the offering of the first animal in the Garden of Eden to the offering of the Lamb of God on Calvary. God rewards obedience and greatly rewards sacrificial obedience.

My Experience

After I graduated with my bachelor's degree, a few friends and I broke our pens and threw them out as a sign that we would never again return to school. About four years later, for some reason, going back to school to obtain a master's degree in business administration (MBA) became the thing to do. As not to feel left out, I registered for the program and hated it. The first chance I got to quit; I seized it.

But then, ten years later, I was sitting in my living room conversing with someone about their MBA application. I clearly heard the Lord tell me to register for the MBA program, too. He also gave me a dream about the school He wanted me to attend. I was unhappy, so I began making my case for why I did not want to return to school—especially for business administration. My primary reason for protesting was that I had answered God's call to full-time ministry. Therefore, returning to school for a business degree did not make sense to me. I could not see how college would fit into my full-time ministry schedule as a teacher of His Word.

I also reminded God that I had tried the program a few years before, but none of the classes made sense to me, and I felt like a fish out of water. In high school, I took economics, which was the closest I got to business studies. I disliked the class so much that I dropped it halfway through the school year.

I wanted the Lord to see that I was not cut out for business-related studies. I reminded Him that I was a pure science student with no interest in arts or business.

It's funny how we try to convince the One who formed us and who knows what He put in us that we cannot be who He is calling us to be. I prayed, hoping the

Lord would change His mind, but He was silent. I have learned that when God has given you some instructions, no amount of fasting, praying, or whining will convince Him to change His instructions. You can either choose to obey or disobey Him.

After failing to persuade God to let me off the hook, I fearfully registered for the program, and I say fearfully because I did not want to knowingly disobey God. Though I was obedient, I didn't enjoy the experience one bit. While going through this program, I struggled a lot and cried many tears. Being in a foreign country with 13 other students from 11 countries was challenging. That meant there were 11 different English-speaking accents. As you can imagine, it was hard to understand my professors and classmates, and I bet they had to work at understanding me.

I desperately wanted to give up, so I came up with what I thought was a persuasive argument. I told the Lord that I had been out of school for so long, I could not possibly make it, and I felt too old to be in that class. Unfortunately for me and my argument, I found out that I was neither the oldest in the class nor the one who had been out of school the longest. I felt stuck because the Lord was not releasing me to walk away, and I was too afraid to be out of His will. I did not want to be like Jonah, who ran from God's will and ended up in the belly of a whale (Jonah 1-4). Besides, I noticed my classmates were struggling too, but none threw in the towel.

In the middle of my pity party, the Spirit of God said to me, "If these non-Christians, who do not know how to obtain mercy and grace from Me, have enough tenacity to stick it out, what is your excuse? What will be your testimony when you quit?" At that, I knew if I could not fly to the finish line, I would have to crawl there, but backing out was not an option.

I finished the program, tears, and all, with abundant divine grace and mercy. God also gave me some miracles along the way, and I viewed them as rewards for my obedience. That program, at that time, was the most challenging assignment I had ever been given. I look back today, 17 years later, and I am so glad I obeyed Him. I did not understand why it was necessary then, but I know now. The knowledge and training I received have helped and are still helping me more than I can measure.

As the Redeemed, sacrificial obedience is required. You must trust God when it does not make sense and when it stretches you beyond your comfort zone. I can personally testify that sacrificial obedience yields excellent dividends. You may sow in tears, but you will reap in joy (Psalm 126:5-6).

When life gets difficult, follow Jesus' example. Concerning our Lord, Hebrews 12:2 says, "Let us fix our eyes on Jesus, the author and perfecter of our faith, who for the joy set before him endured the cross, scorning its shame, and sat down at the right hand of the throne of God."

Complete Obedience

Complete obedience is following through with God's command to you. Doing so pleases our Heavenly Father because bringing things to completion is one of His attributes. Since He completes everything, He starts and always honors His Word, and so should we. God is bound by His Word. The Bible says that God is not a man who lies or a son of man who changes His mind (Numbers 23:19). So then, in complete obedience, we reflect God's image and likeness. As the Redeemed, it is vital that we follow through with our godly commitments.

Incomplete Obedience

Incomplete obedience means fully understanding the Lord's commands and choosing to obey them only partially. Saul, Israel's first king, was partially obedient. He failed to fully comply with divine instructions as they were presented to him by the prophet Samuel. As a result, God rejected Saul, and the rebellious ruler lost his crown (1 Samuel 15:10-23). His incomplete obedience was considered complete disobedience and was even likened to witchcraft. To reiterate an earlier principle discussed in this book, obedience to the Word equates to love for God (John 14:23; 1 John 5:3; 1 John 2:5).

Chapter Eight

The Redeemed as Co-Laborers

Jesus came to Earth to co-labor with the Father and the Holy Spirit to redeem mankind. As the Redeemed, we are co-laborers with the Godhead and have been invited to do three things:

- Enrich Heaven as a fisher of men.
- Help creation maximize its potential.
- Judge both the world and angels.

> *When one of you has a grievance against another, does he dare go to law before the unrighteous instead of the saints? Or do you not know that the saints will judge the world? And if the world is to be judged by you, are you incompetent to try trivial cases? Do you not know that we are to judge angels? How much more, then, matters pertaining to this life!* (1 Corinthians 6:1-4 ESV)

While recruiting His disciples, Jesus said, "Follow me and I will make you fishers of men" (Matthew 4:19). Being "fishers of men" was a significant assignment because God's wealth is not measured by silver, gold, or precious stones in the kingdom of Heaven. After all, these things already belong to Him. God's wealth is measured by souls, as indicated in Scripture:

> *I pray that your hearts will be flooded with light so that you can see something of the future he has called you to share. I want you to realize that God has been made rich because we who are Christ's have been given to him! (Ephesians 1:18 TLB)*

Many are called, but few are chosen (Matthew 22:14). Many people and beings labor for God but not with God (Isaiah 54:16-17; Matthew 7:22-23). To be a co-laborer in the kingdom of God, you must follow His agenda and do things on His terms (Philippians 1:15). Our purpose is to work in unity with God to fulfill His will on Earth and in the lives of those we are called to reach.

Everything revolves around the will of the Father. Jesus did and said only what He saw and heard from the Father. The Holy Spirit is the same way; He does not speak or do anything outside of what the Father says or does (John 15:12-15). If you are a follower of Jesus Christ, abandoning God's agenda will disrupt the peace that comes from being in sync with Him.

You are responsible for continually seeking God's will, communicating with Him, and dwelling in His presence. Your ultimate fulfillment comes from being in alignment with God and making Him the central focus of your existence. Everything you're searching for is found in Him. It is in Him that we live, move, and have our being (Acts 17:28).

How My Journey Began

As a young girl, I invited Jesus into my heart through a song we sang daily at the public school I attended. Here are the lyrics:

> *Into my heart, into my heart*
> *Come into my heart, Lord Jesus*
> *Come in today, come in to stay.*
> *Come into my heart, Lord Jesus.*
> *Amen!*

We sang the above song every morning during assembly, which we had twice daily—at the beginning and end of the school day. To the best of my recollection, the first praise song I ever learned to sing was also at that public school. We sang it daily at the end of the school day. Here are the lyrics:

Now the day is over,
Night is drawing nigh
Shadows of the evening still across the sky
Glory to the Father
Glory to the Son
And to thee blessed Spirit
Blessed three in one. Amen!

That brings back fond memories because I looked forward to singing those songs. We were taught to clasp our hands, put them by our faces, and close our eyes as we sang. I enjoyed my private time with the Godhead. These peaceful moments were sacred to me.

My Home Life

My parents were separated soon after I was born, so I grew up with just my mom in the home. At five years old, the Lord awakened something in me, and I realized God existed. Suddenly, I wanted Him to be in my life and use me as His servant. It was too bad for me; no one attended church in our household, and Sunday was TV Day. I wanted to participate in church so desperately, but being five, my mom would not permit me to go alone. I had to stay home because there was no one to accompany me to Sunday worship.

The closest I got to the church experience was when Jehovah's Witnesses stopped by our house. I eagerly anticipated their visits because they were the only ones sharing information with me about God. They had a book for children called *My Picture Book of Bible Stories*. I longed to have a copy, but I had no one to purchase it.

As God would have it, at seven years old, we moved to a different town where I discovered a Baptist church and another Evangelical church close to the house. Again, I pleaded with my mom to let me go. This time, since the churches were just a stone's throw from where we lived, she agreed! Going to church was the best thing that ever happened to me. Sunday became my favorite day of the week, and I couldn't get enough of church. I could only attend children's church at such a tender age, but I was hungry for more. For that reason, when our service was over, usually before the grownups, I would find my way to the next church and sneak into their adult service.

Unlike me, my mom was deeply involved in traditional African religion at that time. While practitioners of it believe in a Most High God and have a name for Him in all their languages, they also believe in the existence of demigods. They think demigods are appeased by various sacrifices—food offerings or even human sacrifices—to ward off evil.

The required type of sacrifice depends upon what the person is seeking. Also, witchcraft is rampant in the African traditional religion. Usually, non-witches or wizards wanting protection from witchcraft and demonic spirits seek the help of diviners, sorcerers, fortune tellers, and witch doctors. As you can see, this religion follows a lot of idolatrous practices, and they were at odds with my blossoming faith in Christ.

I remember being taught the Ten Commandments at children's church and learning from our teacher that idol worship was a sin against God. The message gripped my heart because I knew my mother was deep into idolatry, so I prayed and asked the Lord to help me present this information to her.

When I returned from church, I summoned the courage to share the Word, but she brushed me off and told me I did not know what I was talking about because I was only a child. I left it at that but remained determined to serve the Lord the Bible way. I knew I did not want to follow in my mother's footsteps. Over time, my faith in God and my pursuit of His ways caused friction between us. I would not participate in idolatrous practices, and at one point, she banned me from attending church services.

The Price

I knew that becoming a Christian would cost me, and I honestly didn't mind the idea of paying a price for my faith. By turning 12, I had already read a lot about Christian martyrs. In my zeal, with a limited amount of knowledge, I asked the Lord to sign me up as one. I wanted to be a martyr for the Lord, so I disobeyed my mother and attended church anyway.

A Catholic church near our house held service around the time my mother would shower when she wasn't at work. I often snuck out to attend their service and hoped to return home before my mother realized I was gone. It worked some days, but other days, I got caught. On those occasions when my mom discovered my disobedience, she punished me in various ways. Sometimes, I was flogged and denied food, or my mother would pronounce curses over me. Yet, none of it fazed me. By the grace of God, the nuns, who knew food might be withheld from me as punishment, had compassion on me and fed me before I returned home. Whenever I was severely punished afterward, I remember finding a place of solitude to rejoice. As one who desired to be a martyr, I counted it a privilege to be punished for my faith.

As I learned the ways of God, I was also taught to pray for my mother's conversion, which became the focus of my prayers. Finally, after 16 years of praying, the answer manifested on Earth. In my early twenties, I was summoned home by my mother, who had something to share with me. For more than two years, she could not sleep at night. Demonic beings would show up every evening to torment her with whippings, head knocks, and other forms of torture. Her crime was living beyond the age allowed under her covenant with them. The terms of this demonic agreement said my mother was supposed to have died before conceiving me. But she objected to dying before her mother, who was still alive at the time.

Mom's Journey to Salvation

For the first two decades of my life, my mother visited a diviner, sorcerer, or witch doctor at least once a week. When she was being tormented every evening, my mother consulted every one of these people. Each one told her to offer different sacrifices, but none worked. She returned to them and asked what else she could do. One of them asked her if she knew of a prayer group because the level of demonic harassment she was facing could only be dealt with through prayer and fasting.

My mother found a church, and the assistant pastor agreed to pray and fast with her. On one of the days, he felt led to pray over some water for her to shower with and recommended some psalms for her to pray with. My mom went home and did as she was told. That night, she slept through the evening for the first time in years. There was no demonic harassment, no flogging, and no banging of her head. The Lord freed her, and that was how my mother returned to the Lord. She got rid of everything associated with idol worship, went to Bible College, and today she pastors a church.

Do You Have Unsaved Loved Ones?

I shared this testimony to encourage anyone with unsaved loved ones. I plead with you not to give up praying for them. Who knows? God may have planted you in that family because He was confident you would intercede for your bloodline. Like Esther in the Bible, you may have been born, saved, and assigned to stand in the gap for your loved ones. Our Heavenly Father is extending an invitation to you. Will you co-labor with Him in the place of prayer for your unsaved loved ones?

As I mentioned, it took about 16 years for me to see the answer to my prayers. Yet, I do not doubt that God worked behind the scenes all 16 years. For one, despite the demons' violent abuse of my mother, they were not permitted to kill her. If they had their way, they would have ended her life. I believe God restrained the enemy because I did not cease to pray.

I also have an older brother who was raised Muslim but became an atheist after he graduated high school.

When my parents' marriage broke down, my brother was taken from my mother, per customary tradition. He was placed with our uncle, a devout Muslim. My brother had a lot of hurt and anger issues toward God and chose to believe that God was nonexistent. I was about two years old when he was removed from us, so I did not grow up with him. After he left, I did not see him again until I was about 14.

When we reconnected, my heart was broken over his bitterness toward God, and I began to pray for his salvation. Some years later, he got stranded in a desert and called out to God. The Lord heard and met him where he was. He accepted Jesus as his Savior and became a worship leader at the church he joined. Since then, he has stumbled some, but not out of his faith in Jesus Christ. At the time of writing, one of my younger brothers is as zealous for Islam as I am for Jesus. I am praying for him, too. I know that the same God who drew my mother and older brother to Himself will do it again in my younger brother's life.

Every Little Bit Counts

In the kingdom of God, every prayer you pray, each thought you think, Word you say, and deed you do for another person—when it aligns with God's will—counts as co-laboring with God. Heaven records these deeds, and God rewards each one. The Bible says it is an injustice for a laborer not to be rewarded for his work (James 5:4). Since God can neither be unjust nor owe any man, He has committed to reward all who co-labor with Him, both in time and eternity.

> *God is not unjust; he will not forget your work and the love you have shown him as you have helped his people and continue to help them. We want each of you to show this same diligence to the very end, in order to make your hope sure. We do not want you to become lazy, but to imitate those who through faith and patience inherit what has been promised.* (Hebrews 6:10-12)

You can tell much about a person in different cultures worldwide based on their wardrobe. In Heaven, your wardrobe will also tell your story. Even your mansion and what part of Heaven you live in will indicate how you co-labored with God while on Earth. Your righteous acts here will determine the fabric of your Heavenly wardrobe.

> *And to her it was granted to be arrayed in fine linen, clean and bright, for the fine linen is the righteous acts of the saints.* (Revelation 19:8-9 NKJV)

To reiterate, every act of obedience to God's Word matters for the Redeemed. You co-labor with God each time you manifest the fruit of the Spirit: love, joy, peace, patience, kindness, goodness, faithfulness, gentleness, and self-control (Galatians 5:22-23). The presence of righteous fruit qualifies you and everyone who is fruitful to receive Heavenly rewards. God made it easy for every person to get in on this.

He even rewards people for seeking Him, whether they find Him or not (Hebrews 11:6). This may explain the many times Jesus has appeared to Muslims who were genuinely seeking Him. It does not matter what religion a person is in the beginning if they sincerely pursue God. Even if they are going down the wrong path to find Jesus, He meets them and points them in the right direction. Anyone who seeks God with all their heart finds Him (Jeremiah 29:13). He draws near to all who draw near to Him (James 4:8).

The Crowns

Apart from your Heavenly wardrobe and mansions, for those who love God, other rewards will tell that person's story for all eternity. Among these Heavenly rewards are crowns. Paul admonished us to run our race here on Earth to win the promised crown (1 Corinthians 9:24; Revelation 3:11). In my book, *Beyond Sonship to*

Friendship, I write more about the Heavenly crowns listed for us in the Bible.

Why should we desire to win the crown? In Heaven, there is a form of worship that requires casting your crown at the feet of Jesus (Revelation 4:10-11). When participating with the 24 elders in such worship, those who have won crowns will have them to lay at the feet of the King of Kings.

Co-laborers in the Heavenly Realms

The Redeemed not only co-labor with God on Earth, but God uses our journey through time to teach Heavenly rulers and authorities about His manifold wisdom (Ephesians 3:10). Your journey through time impacts the residents of the unseen world. You are *that* valuable. Make each day count for eternity. Look out for all the opportunities God presents to you daily and seize them. Be intentional about making the most of each day. Sow towards Heaven.

Chapter Nine

The Redeemed as God's Field

Every time the Redeemed are in a receiving role, they are God's field. People sow into you or water the seeds other laborers have planted. I am God's field to those who sow into my life, but I am God's co-laborer when I sow into the lives of those I am assigned to.

If you are married with children, you are called to sow into your spouse's and your offspring's lives. That is your assignment; they are your field. At the same time, as parents, you must remember that God is their source and primary parent (Psalm 127:3). Make sure you allow Him to sit in the driver's seat on your parental journey (Isaiah 54:13).

For those in ministry, the people you are called to serve are *your* field. If your assignment is in the marketplace, your workplace or business is your field. Though every field or vineyard belongs to God, as a co-laborer with the Godhead, you are called to sow into various fields. Because you are God's field, you are chosen and expected to bear lasting fruit (John 15:16-17). A fruitful field receives God's blessings, but an unproductive field is in danger of being cursed and eventually burned (Hebrews 6:7-8).

God Created Us As Good But Not Perfect

According to Genesis 1, all God made was good. After Eve was added to the equation, God upgraded everything to *very* good (Genesis 1:31). Women, take note: your presence changed the creation status from good to very good!

According to Matthew 5:48, God is perfect. Therefore, in Genesis 1:26, when God said, "Let us make man in our image and likeness," all creation must have expected Adam and Eve to be perfect. But that was not the case; God saw His creation and declared it very good (Genesis 1:31). I can imagine a puzzled look on some of the celestial beings' faces as they wondered why God made man very good and not perfect like Himself.

As I told you earlier, I like envisioning what may have been going on behind the scenes when I read certain accounts of the Bible. In this case, I picture a conversation among the angelic beings. They must have wanted to understand the mystery of why mankind was created to be very good and not perfect.

Remember, through mankind, God is teaching principalities and powers about His manifold wisdom (Ephesians 3:10). I bet the Godhead was excited to unveil this mystery to the celestial beings.

Adam, Eve, and all mankind— including Jesus at birth—were formed and called *very good*. Jesus had to be like us in every way (Hebrews 2:17), but God's intention from the beginning was for us to be perfect as He is perfect. When God called mankind very good, He indicated that humans were a work in progress. His starting point was "very good," but not His finish line! Perfect has always been God's end goal.

As we established, Jesus was perfected through His sacrificial obedience (Hebrews 2:10). He perfected the rest of us through His death on the cross (Hebrews 10:14). Scripture says every good and perfect gift is from above, coming down from the Father of the Heavenly lights (James 1:16). We can't make ourselves perfect. Still, we *can* desire and aim for it (2 Corinthians 13:11). Only the One who started us off as very good can mold us into His image of perfection as we journey through time with Him.

We Are Continuously Being Perfected

We live in a time when the word *perfect* is something we try to avoid. That word appears to stir up negative emotions, and some of us shy away from perfection altogether. Meanwhile, God's goal is to perfect us. The enemy's ploy is to attach negative feelings to words like perfect, righteous, and holy. It is these very words that describe the image and likeness of God! If Satan had his way, he would remove these terms from our vocabulary.

When you accept Jesus as your Lord and personal Savior, the Father makes your spirit perfect. Your soul also starts its renewal process through the Word (Romans 12:1-2), and the Holy Spirit quickens your mortal body (Romans 8:11). You are continuously being perfected. You are being made holy until your mortality gets swallowed up by immortality, and you become immortally perfect—spirit, soul, and body. This is the true reflection of the image and likeness of God and the fulfillment of Genesis 1:26.

Right now, the Redeemed are spirits that are saved with souls that are *being* saved, and we live inside bodies that will *be* saved at the renewal of all things. When we transition out of time, our current clay-sourced body won't go to God's Heaven. At the renewal of all things, our bodies will be transformed by God's power and redesigned to live on the new Earth with God forever. Think of it this way: we are clothed with the right body for the realm we live in. Our current body is designed for a terrestrial realm. At the appointed time, God will recreate it for the celestial realms. You may ask, *why can't we remain in the same body?* Well, God likes newness. He will make a new heaven and Earth, so it does not surprise me that He gives us new bodies for the new Earth (Revelation 21:1).

Why Can't Satan Be Redeemed?

Have you ever wondered why Satan cannot be redeemed? From the very beginning, he was created perfect (Ezekiel 28:12). Therefore, when Satan sinned, nothing else could be done for him. When God finishes a thing, no one can add to it or improve upon His final product. Hence, the writer of Hebrews warns us. If we fall away from the faith after we have been enlightened, tasted of the Heavenly gift, communed with the Holy Spirit, and experienced the goodness of the Word, it is impossible to be brought back to repentance (Hebrews 6:4-6).

Each time you declare that *I am perfect, and I am being made holy* (Hebrews 10:14), you remind Satan of what he lost and what you gained. My guess is he can't stand that. Perfection, holiness, righteousness, and repentance hurt the kingdom of darkness. Satan was with God for eons before he was cast out of Heaven. He has enough history with God to know this: The Lord would not create something in His image and likeness only to make it very good and stop there.

Yet, when Satan saw that God's creation was not perfect, in his pride, I imagine him saying, "*Good and very good? What's up with that? Whatever happened to perfect? Did you stop making them? The perfect ones let You down, and You think these very good ones will be loyal to You and serve You forever? I thought you were going to make this hard on me. I successfully deceived a chunk of Your perfectly created angels, and You think these very good humans will be a match for me? Wow, I would have sworn You were smarter than that!*"

Next, I envision the holy angels reporting to God the details of Satan's boastful rant and God sitting on His throne laughing (Psalm 2). In his ignorance, Satan did not realize it was a setup! He should have been more afraid of the world's less-than-perfect, weak, and foolish things. He did not know this was God's strategy to destroy his wisdom and frustrate his intelligence (1 Corinthian 25:19). Satan was unaware that what appeared weak and foolish was anything but. Consider the crucifixion of Christ and how He died in weakness but was raised in glorious power.

> *But God chose the foolish things of the world to shame the wise; God chose the weak things of the world to shame the strong. He chose the lowly things of this world and the despised things--and the things that are not--to nullify*

the things that are, so that no one may boast before him. (1 Corinthians 1:27-29)

Did you notice that the Heaven and Earth God created in Genesis 1:1 were not created sin-proof? I know this because Satan, who is sin-personified, was given access to Adam and Eve. Can you imagine how shocked he must have been on his first visit to Earth? No angels stopped him. No lightning or thunder struck him down. I suspect he returned to his crew in total disbelief that he could roam the Earth unhindered. I guess after a few trips with no opposition, he figured it was time to come up with a plan to take the man out and rule the world.

Even though sin was allowed on Earth, Satan had no legal right to destroy the Earth because no sin had yet been found in Adam and Eve, the Earth's acting rulers. God has guaranteed a new, sin-proof Heaven and Earth in our future. It will not be very good; it will be perfect (Revelation 21:1,27)! Before Satan ever attempted his evil scheme, God knew every move he would make, and the Father already had a plan of redemption in place. Considering this, it is fitting that, in Scripture, Jesus is called the Lamb that was slain before the foundations of the world (Revelation 13:8).

Chapter Ten

The Redeemed as Intercessors

When God created mankind, He had in mind a kingdom of priests, both male and female. In Leviticus 7:8, when an animal was slaughtered by the priest as a guilt offering to God, the animal's skin was one of the parts given to the priest as his share. If God only wanted *males* to be priests, He could have given Adam the garments of skin and made something else for Eve to wear. But Genesis 3:21 says, "The LORD God made garments of skin for Adam and his wife and clothed them."

By giving Adam and Eve the animal skin, which is reserved for priests in the Bible, it seems like God was making a statement about His intention for the redeemed priests. He could have made clothes out of nothing or some other material altogether. But in keeping with His nature, God did something that spoke of what was to come. Under the Leviticus covenant, only males could be priests. Still, before the Levitical priesthood, the Father wanted the whole nation as a kingdom of priests (Exodus 19:6). Sadly, the Israelites broke the covenant when they turned away from God and worshiped the golden calf. Afterward, God rejected them as priests and chose only the Levites to serve in the priesthood.

Through the prophet Isaiah, the Father began to speak of a coming priesthood that was not all male. It would be made up of the poor, those who had been healed of a broken heart, former captives who had been freed, and previous mourners who were comforted, and they would be called "oaks of righteousness." This priesthood would stand in the gap for restoring their bloodline (Isaiah 61:1-5).

> *They will rebuild the ancient ruins and restore the places long devastated; they will renew the ruined cities that have been devastated for generations. Aliens will shepherd your flocks; foreigners will work your fields and vineyards. And you will be called priests of the LORD, you will be named ministers of our God. (Isaiah 61:4-6)*

Jesus purchased a kingdom of priests with His blood. This fulfilled the desire of the Father's heart (Revelation 5:10; 20:6) and the prophecy in Isaiah 61:6. Peter confirmed this by calling the Redeemed *a royal priesthood* (1 Peter 2:9). You are a part of that royal priesthood. Jesus is our High Priest after the order of Melchizedek. He has the authority of both a priest and a king, so we get an even better deal than the Levitical priesthood. It is the same deal that God intended for us back in Genesis.

A priest's job description includes ministering to God, interceding for others, teaching Scripture, offering gifts and sacrifices to God, and settling legal matters.

> *For every high priest chosen from among men is appointed to act on behalf of men in relation to God, to offer gifts and sacrifices for sins.* (Hebrews 5:1 ESV)

> But to the elders he said, "Wait here for us until we return to you. And behold, Aaron and Hur are with you; whoever has a legal matter, let him approach them." (Exodus 24:14 NASB95)

Additionally, our priesthood is not required to offer animal sacrifices. Instead, we offer sacrificial obedience (Hebrews 5:8-10), our bodies (Romans 12:1), and praises (Hebrews 13:15).

Dimensions of Prayer

Learning how to pray is necessary to be effective in our role as priests. I define prayer as communicating with God. Jesus, when preparing His disciples for their assignment, taught them how to pray. Prayer is something you learn; it can and should be taught. John also taught his disciples to pray (Luke 11:1). I began learning to pray by reading the Book of Psalms. Later, I progressed to using prayer books. I am thankful for those who graciously took the time to publish them because I was greatly helped.

When I fellowshipped with other believers, I continued growing in my understanding of prayer, and I am still learning to this day.

God has given the Redeemed the gift of praying in three languages: the language of men, the language of angels (1 Corinthians 13:1), and the language of God, also called unknown tongues— which are unknown to all but God (1 Corinthians 14:2). It behooves us to use all the tools God has made available to us. We would be short selling ourselves to pick and choose from His supply of resources. Get them all because the One that made them available knows best. Moreover, speaking in other tongues is one of the signs that Jesus said would follow those who believe in Him (Mark 16:17-18). Most people receive the gift of tongues when they get baptized in the Holy Spirit (Acts 19:6). Any believer can ask for the gift.

God As Father

Jesus taught His disciples three dimensions of prayer: approaching God as Father, friend, and judge. In The Lord's Prayer, Jesus taught His disciples how to approach God as Father.

> *In this manner, therefore, pray: Our Father in Heaven, Hallowed be Your name. Your kingdom come. Your will be done on earth as it is in Heaven. Give us this day our daily bread. And forgive us our debts, as we forgive our debtors. And do not lead us into temptation but deliver us from the evil one. For Yours is the kingdom and the power and the glory forever. Amen. (Matthew 6:9-13 NKJV)*

I love so many things about this prayer. As royal priests, we must know God as our Father, the source of who we are. Addressing our prayers to our Father in Heaven distinguishes Him from any other father figure we may have. There is so much to write about this prayer, but for the purpose of this book, I will limit myself to verses nine and eleven. I do not consider this passage of Scripture a mere prayer pattern; to me, it *is* a prayer.

Recently, I noticed that The Lord's Prayer is not an "I" or "me" prayer. This is an "us" kind of prayer. This is the most strategic and comprehensive prayer I have ever heard. As a person who loves efficient and effective strategies, I greatly enjoy this prayer. It helps me maximize time, opportunities, and potential.

Matthew 6:9

On this occasion, Jesus did not teach His disciples to pray *My Father*; He taught them to say *our Father*.

This teaches us to consider others when we approach God as Father and avoid being self-centered. Being mindful that God is not only *your* Father but also the Father of other people will influence your response to His sovereignty—especially when He chooses not to answer in the way you hoped He would.

As a nursing home administrator, eleven department heads reported directly to me. When a department head requested something for their unit, I had to consider all eleven departments when deciding whether to grant or deny their request. It was my responsibility as the head of that organization to ensure that the whole building remained in sync with our goals. Sometimes, I had to deny requests because of the impact they would have on the other departments.

As believers, we are all micro-units under one big unit called the Body of Christ. We are each connected directly or indirectly. Together, we participate in a program initiated and run by God called *time*. God is head over all. Each time He responds to us, He considers the impact His response will have on every unit in the Body. He is *our* Father, not just *yours* or *mine*.

When I was told my 16-year-old son was not going to make it after a failed bone marrow transplant, I cried out to God to spare his life. He was just three weeks shy of his 17th birthday. There were several other times he could have died, but God spared him. There were multiple times I could have died, but God sovereignly spared my life. I have enough history with God to know that nothing is too hard for Him. I don't know why the answer was not yes, this time. However, I do know that God took everything and everyone into consideration when He chose to receive my son back to Himself.

This knowledge has kept me worshipping God despite the answer I got. When you know God as *our* Father, you will discover that everything He does and allows is righteous, love-driven, and always in the best interest of all parties concerned.

Matthew 6:11

"Give us this day our daily bread." Wow, what a strategy. In one breath, I can pray for myself and my entire bloodline. As a priest, I am appointed to represent man, including those connected to me by blood, marriage, faith, and assignments. We are commanded to pray for all in authority and each other. How long would it take me to fulfill my obligation to pray for all connected to me by faith without this prayer? I don't know about you, but one of my biggest frustrations as I travel through time is the limitation that our 24-hour day imposes. I find that it isn't enough time to do all I'd love to do on each given day. Consequently, I am a lifetime student of the school of time management.

As a royal priest, this prayer strategy enables me to stand in the gap for nations in one breath! Through this "us" strategy, I can influence what is going on in the White House, Saudi Arabia, Iran, and practically anywhere in the world by carrying them in my heart as I pray to *our* Father.

> *Whenever Aaron enters the Holy Place, he will bear the names of the sons of Israel over his heart on the breast piece of decision as a continuing memorial before the LORD. (Exodus 28:29)*

When I plead with the Father to *give us this day our daily bread*, I take the limits off Him. When I say these words, I ask Him for provision based on His glorious riches. I am praying per His agenda for that day, which could include God raining down manna from Heaven if that is what the situation requires. My knowledge of what each day will bring is limited. I don't see the end from the beginning, but He does! When I ask based on what I think my day is going to be like, I short-change myself.

Have you ever had one of those I-*didn't-see-that-coming* days? Sometimes, I can't ask the right thing because I need more information about what is happening or what will happen. But when I pray, *give us this day our daily bread*; I don't have to know everything—or anything at all—because I am petitioning an all-knowing being. He is the Omniscient God. My responsibility as a royal priest is to carry the names of the people, places, and things in my heart into the holy place of prayer. By praying to *give us this day our daily bread*, I activate the release of angels into those circumstances because angels exist to execute God's counsel on earth.

As A Friend

Then he said to them, "Suppose one of you has a friend, and he goes to him at midnight and says, 'Friend, lend me three loaves of bread because a friend of mine on a journey has come to me, and I have nothing to set before him." Then the one inside answers, "Don't bother me. The door is already locked, and my children are with me in bed. I can't get up and give you anything." I tell you, though he will not get up and give him the bread because he is his friend, yet because of the man's boldness he will get up and give him as much as he needs. So, I say to you: Ask and it will be given to you; seek and you will find; knock and the door will be opened to you. (Luke 11:5-9)

In this Scripture, Jesus taught His disciples to approach God as a friend on behalf of another friend. Remember, priests are appointed to represent not just themselves but others. What jumped off the page for me is a powerful principle: Jesus is teaching us that we have a role to play in seeing God's Kingdom come, and His will be done on earth as it is in Heaven. Jesus isn't going to do everything without our involvement. We must do our part with the same persistence demonstrated by the friend in the above Bible passage.

How badly do you hunger to see God's will done? How badly do you want to see His kingdom come? How badly do you want to see what He has promised in His word become a reality in your life? How badly do you want the needs of those assigned to you met? How hungry are you for righteousness?

If you want it badly enough, you will get it. Jesus said, "Blessed are those who hunger and thirst for righteousness for they shall be full" (Matthew 5:6). Jesus taught His disciples to ask and keep asking, seek and keep seeking, and knock and keep knocking until the answer is released.

Chapter Eleven

Approaching God as Judge

After Jesus taught His disciples to approach God as a friend on behalf of others, He introduced the idea of asking for the Holy Spirit.

> *Which of you fathers, if your son asks for a fish, will give him a snake instead? Or if he asks for an egg, will give him a scorpion? If you then, though you are evil, know how to give good gifts to your children, how much more will your Father in Heaven give the Holy Spirit to those who ask him! (Luke 11:11-13)*

Jesus is a genius! The disciples needed to grasp the first lesson before Jesus could teach them to tap into the next dimension of prayer: approaching God as a judge. Asking for the Holy Spirit first is essential for this reason: you will need an advocate if you are going to show up before God, the judge. The Holy Spirit is an advocate (John 14:26)

In most countries that use this terminology, an advocate is a high-ranking lawyer rather than an entry-level attorney. In the UK's legal system, advocates can be likened to a queen's counsel (QC). As a royal priesthood, the Redeemed are like junior lawyers, and the Holy Spirit is the senior advocate. If you are going to court against an enemy more knowledgeable and experienced than you, it is highly recommended that you go with the Holy Spirit.

No man in their earthly form, without the power of the Holy Spirit, is a match for Satan. Remember, he was a covering cherub (Ezekiel 28:14). The Bible says, concerning the Father, that holiness adorns His house. Righteousness and justice are the foundations of His throne. Bear that in mind as we continue our journey into this third dimension of prayer.

The Judge That Is Eager to Bring Justice

In the parable of the Persistent Widow, Jesus emphasized the need for persistence in prayer and the necessity of approaching God as a judge. This invariably leads to the need to know how to operate in the courts of Heaven.

> *Then Jesus told his disciples a parable to show them that they should always pray and not give*

> up. He said: "In a certain town there was a judge who neither feared God nor cared about men. And there was a widow in that town who kept coming to him with the plea, 'Grant me justice against my adversary.' "For some time he refused. But finally, he said to himself, 'Even though I don't fear God or care about men, yet because this widow keeps bothering me, I will see that she gets justice, so that she won't eventually wear me out with her coming!'" And the Lord said, "Listen to what the unjust judge says. And will not God bring about justice for his chosen ones, who cry out to him day and night? Will he keep putting them off? I tell you; he will see that they get justice, and quickly. (Luke 18:1-8)

Did you notice in this passage that God, unlike the unjust judge, is eager to bring justice for His chosen ones? Let's look at Ecclesiastes 8:6:

> "For there is a proper time and procedure for every matter, though a man's misery weighs heavily upon him."

There is a time to approach God as Father and friend but also to switch gears and approach Him as a judge. Hebrews 12:23 says you can come to God, the judge of all men. You must appear in His courtroom to approach the Father as a judge. Remember, every matter has a proper time, place, and procedure. Who do you take with you to approach God as the judge? You take your advocate, the Holy Spirit, and your Redeemer, Jesus Christ. To re-emphasize, this is why Jesus taught the disciples to ask for the Holy Spirit before teaching them to approach God as a judge. There are no insignificant details or placements in the Bible!

You know God has courtrooms, right? Where do judges carry out their business? In a courtroom. Since God is a judge, it is a given that He has courtrooms. There are so many Scriptures about God operating in a courtroom setting. I will provide you with three: Daniel 7:9-10, Zechariah 3:1-7, and Psalm 82:1-2.

> *God stands up to open Heaven's court. He pronounces judgment on the judges. How long will you judges refuse to listen to the evidence? How long will you shower special favors on the wicked? (Psalm 82:1-2 TLB)*

Heavenly Courtrooms

Did you know that our Heavenly Father has a courtroom that can hold over 100 million people in one setting (Daniel 7:9-10)? God has realms in the heavens where His court proceedings are held, and Satan and his team have access to some of these courts (Zechariah 3:1-2). To some extent, the legal systems on Earth mimic the courts of Heaven, but God's courtroom is not limited to the Heavenly realms. If He was only a judge, He'd need to be in a specific location to conduct business. Still, because He is a kingly judge, He can hold court wherever He goes. The first place we see God as a judge is on Earth, in the Garden of Eden (Genesis 3:8-19).

He Paid For Our Perfection

When Jesus died on the cross, He paid the total price for our redemption and restoration. When man sinned in Eden, we did not fall short of mercy or grace, but we fell short of God's glory (Romans 3:23). Man, now operates at a lower level of glory than God originally intended, and this is the cause of all the limitations we experience and the brokenness of the world around us.

Restoration of the glory is the key to healing the division we see in Christ's body and unlocking unity. Satan wants the church to remain fragmented; the complete unity of the body of Christ is one of the greatest threats to him. Unification of the church would reveal to the whole world that Jesus was indeed sent by the Father, and the body of Christ would know the depths of the Father's love in a way it never has before (John 17:22-23).

Do you know Jesus paid for us to walk in divine health? Do you know Jesus paid in full for us to have a sound mind? How much of what Jesus paid for have you obtained? Are there things you've read about in the Word of God, which have been prophesied over you, that you have prayed about, fasted over, bound, loosed, and cast out— and yet nothing is shifting? Are there unpleasant things that seem to run in your bloodline? Is there an adverse history that appears to be repeating itself, even after you have fasted and prayed? If you have answered yes to any of these questions, Satan may have a legal right to operate in that area of your life, and he may have a lawsuit against you in the courts of Heaven.

If that is the case, it's time to approach your Heavenly Father as the judge. You may ask, *why do I have to go to court? Why won't Jesus just take care of everything?* It's because there are rules and protocols of engagement in the realm of the spirit. The Bible says there is a time and procedure for every matter (Ecclesiastes 8:6), and Jesus lives to make intercession for us. There are countless things Jesus and the Holy Spirit do for us that we may never know until we arrive in Heaven. Still, some processes also call for our active participation.

Why Go To Court?

1) The kingdom of God is a nation at war.

A war started before time began when Lucifer, now called Satan, tried to overthrow God. The war is closer to its end today than yesterday (Revelation 12:7-9).

2) The enemy brings litigation against you to slow you down or hold you back.

We go to court to strip him of his legal right to do that to us.

> *Since we have such a huge crowd of men of faith watching us from the grandstands, let us strip off anything that slows us down or holds us back, and especially those sins that wrap themselves so tightly around our feet and trip us up; and let us run with patience the particular race that God has set before us.* (Hebrews 12:1. TLB)

3) Satan is our legal opponent.

If you have a legal opponent, you had better know your way to the courthouse and how to operate there.

> *Be sober, be vigilant, because your adversary, the devil, walks about like a roaring lion,*

seeking whom he may devour. (1 Peter 5:8 NKJV)

In the Hebrew language, Satan means adversary. In the New Testament, the word adversary means one who brings a lawsuit against another (Matthew 5:25, 1 Peter 5:8), one who demands a trial, or one who insists that a person be given up for torture or punishment, as in Peter's case in Luke 22:31-32. Satan is a prosecuting attorney. In the book of Job, when asked where he had come from, Satan reported that he had been roaming the Earth, going back and forth in it (Job 2: 1-2). Peter, however, warned us that Satan is not roaming the Earth aimlessly. He seeks someone to bring charges against and devour (1 Peter 5:8).

Since Satan was kicked out of Heaven as a covering cherub, it does not surprise me that he is a prosecuting attorney. But the good news is that Satan cannot devour at random. He must have a legal right to do so. Except for God picking a fight with Satan and the Lord teaching a generational lesson, as in the case of Job, only two things give Satan the legal right to execute his sinister plan: sin and our ignorance (Hosea 4:6).

Sin Gives Satan A Legal Right

Sin entered the world and the Garden of Eden through Satan. Still, he could not devour anything until he successfully lured mankind into sin. Sin empowers our adversary and his armies. If you remove sin, Satan loses his legal right to dwell there. On the contrary, if sin is found inside a person, place, or thing, Satan's occupancy is legal, and you can't cast him out. You cannot arrest someone who is not trespassing or breaking the law. For captives to be freed, you must make the strongman holding them captive an illegal trespasser (Matthew 12:29). The way to bind Satan is by making him illegal.

4) Going to court is necessary.

If going to court was unnecessary, Jesus would not have taught the disciples to approach God as a judge to receive justice.

5) We are in training to rule with Him as judges.

As co-laboring intercessors, we may start out as priests, but the end goal is to be a judge. To my knowledge, no one recently graduated from law school instantly becomes a judge. Before ascending to the judge's bench, you must practice law for a specified period. In the same way, we must prepare for our future role as judges by operating in the courts of Heaven while living on Earth. In the book of Revelation, Jesus promised that those who overcome will be given authority over nations (Revelation 2:26). If you can't be a priest, how will you be a king and a judge?

    6) Why go to court? Because one day in His courts is better than a thousand outside.

For a day in Your courts is better than a thousand outside. I would rather stand at the threshold of the house of my God Than dwell in the tents of wickedness. (Psalms 84:10 NASB95)

How to Illegalize Satan

To make Satan illegal, you must intentionally remove sin; it does not go away on its own. Whether it is your sin or the sins of those in your bloodline, somebody must stand in the gap to deal with it, just as Daniel did for his people. To remove sin, the blood of Jesus must be applied. To apply the blood, there must be confession and repentance. Repentance, which is the act of turning to face and obeying the Word, binds Satan. The Word is a letter; you can read Him. The Word is a message; you can hear Him. The Word is a person; you can touch and talk to Him. In all three manifestations of the Word, if you don't follow Jesus, history will repeat itself. You need to yield to the Word to maintain your victory.

Court Judgements

After Calvary, Jesus obtained a judgment against sin and death. Everything we need for life and godliness is contained within that judgment obtained in the Heavenly courts (2 Peter 1:3). Note that there are aspects of that judgment that you can only enforce on the Earth if you take certain steps.

Sometimes, you must return to the courts to ask for an enforcement order.

Jurisdiction

If you have been through a divorce with children involved, you can relate to my story. Once, I had a judgment from a court in Scotland that granted me full custody of my children. While living in Scotland, my children were taken to Africa. In my ignorance, I thought I could just go pick them up from Africa with the decree in hand, but I soon discovered that the legal system doesn't work that way. I could not just fly into the African Country where they were and pick them up. I had to appear in the nation's court and request an order to enforce the favorable judgment I received in Scotland. I learned that a judgment from another country was not automatically enforceable.

The children were taken to Canada as that case was still going on. I flew into Canada with the judgment from Scotland and thought I could go to the police and have them escort me to pick up my son. I was wrong—again. The police said I had to go to the courts in Canada to obtain an order authorizing the police to enforce that judgment from Scotland. Eight years passed since the time the judgment was obtained and when it was finally enforced.

After Jesus fully paid for the remission of our sins, He obtained a judgment for the Redeemed that contains every promised blessing in the Bible. Some of us are not walking in the fullness of God's blessings because we have not requested that the judgment obtained in Heaven be enforced in the earthly realm. We are living under the assumption that just because we have the decree in hand, all those benefits tied to it should automatically be released to us. That is not always the case, especially when your legal opponent does not let his captives go free except by force. There are times when God sovereignly blesses us. There are also times when He waits for us to show up in court and request the enforcement of the judgment Jesus obtained by His blood.

Initiating Proceedings

The Redeemed can initiate proceedings in the courts of Heaven (Luke 18:7). Sometimes, God initiates the proceedings. For example, in the Garden of Eden, God summoned Adam and Eve to court (Genesis 3:8-19). Satan can also file a case against a person in the courts of Heaven. For instance, he had a case against Joshua, the high priest (Zechariah 3:1), and the apostle Peter (Luke 22:3132).

> *Then he showed me Joshua the high priest standing before the angel of the LORD, and Satan standing at his right side to accuse him. (Zechariah 3:1)*

How Do I Approach God as Judge?

There are many books on Amazon about the courts of Heaven. Dr. Ron Horner and Robert Henderson have excellent books on this subject. They go into more detail about how to operate in that realm. There are also YouTube videos on this subject matter. I highly recommend you get some of these materials and read up on the subject, as I will not cover it extensively in this book. I aim to create awareness of the courts of Heaven and the need to learn how to operate in them.

Every nation on Earth has a court system with different courts for various matters. This system on Earth is patterned after Heaven's system; there are multiple courts in Heaven, too. Regardless of which court your case will be presented in, certain principles apply each time you approach God as a judge.

Stand On a Platform of Repentance

No matter who initiated the proceeding, you are guaranteed victory if you approach God as a judge on a platform of repentance. When you have turned away from your sin, it is illegal for the enemy to use it against you (Ezekiel 33:14-16). The Bible says, "If we confess our sins, He is faithful and just to forgive us." Every sin placed under Jesus's blood is wholly atoned for and cleansed forever.

Jesus informed us that if an adversary is taking us to court, we should make peace with him before we appear before the judge (Matthew 5:25). If Satan is taking us to court, that is not the time to start binding or losing him. Whatever facts he has against you, accept them, confess, and repent of them, with him as a witness, *before* you show up in court. If you are already in court and a matter that you were not aware of (or that you are aware of but have not dealt with) is brought up, confess and repent.

Can you imagine what would have happened in Eden if Adam and Eve had taken responsibility for their sin, confessed, and asked for forgiveness instead of shifting blame? I strongly believe mankind would have been on a different path. There would still have been consequences for their sin, but the damage would not have been this bad. Every time there is repentance, the enemy loses his legal ground to keep you imprisoned. Even God cannot condemn a repentant sinner.

My First Courtroom Experience

I was in a city when an angel of the Lord came up to me and informed me that I had been summoned to appear before the Lord in a court. I asked the angel to give me a few minutes to examine myself, and he granted my request. I remember falling on my face and examining my conscience for any unconfessed sin. Soon, the angel returned to say it was time to go. Immediately, my spirit left my body. I could see my body lying on the ground as we started ascending toward Heaven on a very busy stairway.

When we arrived in the courtroom, Jesus was seated as a judge with my heart in His hands. There was another person there whose role was to open my book and read aloud everything recorded inside. I realized this was a record of all my wrongdoings. As this person flipped through each page, I observed that each one was as white as snow. He suddenly flipped to a page with a sentence written on it and read aloud what was recorded. Instantly, I recalled what it was—a sin I had committed and said I would repent, but I didn't because I forgot.

My initial response was to make an excuse, but then I changed my mind and decided to take responsibility. I looked to the Lord and said, "You are just in all You do. I plead for mercy." This person continued to flip through all the pages until he reached the end. Apart from that page, all the other pages were white as wool. At once, I understood the Scripture that says, "Even if our sins are as red as scarlet, he will wash us as white as snow" (Isaiah 1:18). I saw that when we confess our sins, His blood truly washes them away (1 John 1:9). I also learned that unconfessed sins remain. Without the confession of sin, there is no forgiveness.

There are several books in Heaven about every single human on Earth. Some books contain a record of our righteous deeds and our sinful acts. The Bible teaches that these books will be opened when we stand before the judge of mankind (Revelation 20:12). Throughout the proceedings, the Lord never took His eyes off my heart He was holding in His hands. When the person was done reading my book, the Lord looked up and started talking to me about how appreciative He was of my heart and my love for the Father.

I later learned that I was in the courtroom of commissioning to receive my assignment. Initially, I did not want to return to the Earth, but I heard the audience pleading for me to go back and turn people back to the Lord. I still did not want to leave, but the Lord said I had to. When the proceedings were finished, the angel escorted me back to Earth, where my body was lying. While I was gone, another angel was watching over my body. After my trip to the court of Heaven was over, my spirit slid back into my body. With that, I got up and continued on my way. When you approach God as a judge, go with a repentant heart.

The Courtroom of Litigation

As a royal priesthood, we can initiate a proceeding in court on behalf of others, particularly if they are assigned to us. Once, I was upstairs at our house praying, taking my husband's case to the courts of Heaven. Simultaneously, he was downstairs reading his Bible and found himself transported into a Heavenly courtroom. The Father was seated as the judge, and others sat in the courtroom. Jesus was seated as well but as a witness. Satan was also there, bringing accusations against my husband. As the enemy spoke, the Holy Spirit, my husband's advocate, refuted the accuser.

Jesus was there confirming everything the Holy Spirit stated on behalf of my husband.

My husband did not even know I was upstairs interceding for him while he was having this experience. He only told me about his supernatural encounter later that day. That's when I revealed that I, too, had been in the courts of Heaven. On this occasion, my husband was in the courtroom of litigation. Ever since we started showing up in the courts of Heaven, we have seen a lot of positive shifts in our lives and those connected to us by blood and assignment. Jesus informed His disciples that they would approach the Father to ask for things in His name after He returned to the Father.

> *In that day you will ask in my name. I am not saying that I will ask the Father on your behalf. No, the Father himself loves you because you have loved me and have believed that I came from God. (John 16:26-27 NIV)*

Testimonies

A close friend of ours received a call that her cousin, who was fighting cancer, was going to die within an hour. The doctors had pulled the plugs. She called us to request that we go to the courts on her behalf to petition for her cousin to be granted three hours to allow those traveling from out of state to say their goodbyes. My husband and I took the case to the courts of heaven.

Instead of petitioning for three hours, we were inspired by the Holy Spirit to petition for her to complete the number of days that were appointed to her by God before she was conceived in her mother's womb, based on Psalm 139:13-16. Satan, the adversary, was also in court to oppose us. These were our early days of learning to operate within the courts of heaven. We did not know much, but Yeshua was with us as our Senior advocate. Satan argued that she was already a believer and would go straight to heaven if she died, so why prolong her days on earth? It was quite a contention.

We called for her records as a witness. The records, which were rolls and rolls of scrolls, were brought in. The scrolls contained:

- Records of her acts of kindness.
- Words of encouragement she had spoken to people.
- The many lives she had touched.

The adversary requested that the records of her sins be presented. Those scrolls were brought in and presented to the Judge. Judge Elohim examined the scrolls, and it was all white as snow. Before the hearing, we had stood in the gap for her based on John 20:21-23. We remitted every record of sin against her, so when her records were presented, there was nothing on them because they had been placed under the blood of the Lamb of God.

Satan insisted that the Judge scrutinize the scrolls and look more intently, hoping that he would find something. Judge Elohim answered Satan, saying, "There is nothing to be found."

Satan retorted, "So you are going to extend her life?" Yeshua stepped in at that point. He stated, "This is not about extending her life. This is a petition for her to live out the number of days she was appointed before she was conceived." Satan argued again, "What difference does it make? She's coming to heaven anyway!" Yeshua responded, "Even if it is one more act of kindness she can do, it will be well worth it." Judge Elohim granted our petition.

That was quite an experience for me. I learned a lot from that court session. I saw how real it is when sins are deleted by the blood of Yeshua. I gained a better appreciation for acts of kindness and words of encouragement sowed into the lives of others. I realize Satan is inconvenienced by every believer on earth. When believers transition out of time, it's one less thorn in his flesh. Satan wants to steal as many seconds, minutes, hours, days, weeks, months, or years as he can steal from everyone if allowed to do so.

We later learned that 50 years was appointed to our friend's cousin. At the time of this court case, she was three weeks short of her fiftieth birthday. Satan wanted to rob her of the last weeks appointed unto her.

Our friend's cousin did not die within the hour as expected by the doctors, though the life support had been pulled. She bounced back. All her loved ones who flew in from out of state could see her and spend some days with her. She was discharged from the hospital to a rehabilitation center. I was able to travel with my friend to visit her. We prayed and had communion with her. We led her in prayer to stand in the gap for her bloodline. She had a cousin she wanted to see saved. We prayed for that. She did more acts of kindness. On the morning of her fiftieth birthday, she took her last breath, having completed the number of days appointed unto her in time. Yeshua paid in full for those fifty years. He deserved the return on His investment. He won!

A few weeks after she transitioned out of time, the cousin she longed to see saved gave his life to Christ. Hallelujah!

There was another brother in Christ who had battled cancer for years. He beat it, and then it returned. This time, he was sent home with about three weeks to live. We went to the courts on his behalf. Having learned from our previous court case, we decided to ask for an extension of this brother's life beyond what he was appointed before he was conceived. The Judge did not grant our petition as requested. We were granted the number of days originally appointed unto this brother. He lived for six months beyond medical expectations.

This was another case of Satan wanting to rob what he could if allowed. It is vital for the Redeemed to go to the courts and make their wishes known as to how long they want to live on earth. The minimum should be what was written in your book before you were conceived (Psalm 139:13-16). There is also room for extension. Paul the Apostle had an extension upon request (Philippians 1:21-26). You can at least ask.

Chapter Twelve

The Redeemed as the Most Resourced Beings on Earth

As children of God, the Redeemed have access to the most available resources. According to 2 Peter 1:3, God has deposited everything we need for life and godliness within us by His divine power. This is an incredible gift!

Yeshua (Jesus) said that just as the Father sent Him into the world, He is also sending us (John 20:21-23). The Father sent Yeshua with an army of angels at His disposal - more than 12 legions, which would have comprised over 72,000 angels if needed (Matthew 26:53). As heirs to Salvation, we are told that angels are ministering spirits sent to serve us (Hebrews 1:14).

It is essential to bear in mind that angels are mighty beings. One angel was able to kill 185,000 Assyrian soldiers (2 Kings 19:35). When David sinned against God, only one angel was sent to execute judgment on Israel, resulting in the death of 70,000 Israelites (1 Chronicles 21:15).

Yeshua had over 72,000 angels at His disposal to accomplish His work on earth. He said that the Redeemed would do the works He did and more (John 14:12). No one doing the work of Yeshua has fewer angels available to them than He did while on earth (1 John 4:17-21). However, Yeshua made it clear that to activate the angels' services, He had to submit a request to His Father (Matthew 26:53).

The Bible reminds us that we often lack because we fail to ask (James 4:2). Therefore, not all resources are automatically dispensed to the Redeemed. Many resources require our active participation in the form of submitting a request. This highlights the importance of our personal engagement in accessing the resources available to us.

Angels are a significant part of the resources that our Heavenly Father has made available to those who have been Redeemed by His Son. Different categories and rankings of angels are assigned to us, and stars are also part of our troops. Remember, Yeshua's star led the wise men with the resources they needed to come to worship Him in Bethlehem (Matthew 2:1-2). The stars fought with Deborah against Sisera (Judges 5:20). Galaxies of stars might be gifted to some people (Revelation 2:28), as God loves to give according to His capacity. He told Abraham to look up to the heavens and count the stars if he could, for that's how numerous his descendants would be (Genesis 15:5). This underscores the role of angels as a significant part of the resources available to us.

Scrolls are also part of our troops (Zechariah 5:1-4). Everything in God's arsenal is part of our weapons of warfare (Jeremiah 50:25). All these resources are available to the Redeemed who ask.

The Lord has taught us to wear His armor daily and ask our angels to draw near us. We ask that all our troops draw near to their various places of assignment and be in active service. We stand in the gap for all our realms, angels, and troops, requesting that the Father supply all their needs according to His glorious riches in Christ Yeshua. We ask that He clothe us individually and corporately with His armor of light in and out of time. We request reinforcement for all our realms, angels, and troops with higher-ranking angels as needed for that day and season.

The Lord taught us to request that our troops be granted dominance in the regions of their assignment over other entities. The angel that was sent to bring the answer to Daniel's prayer was detained by the prince of Persia, who dominated that region (Daniel 10:13-14). We ask that our angels and troops check in with the Holy

Spirit for their instructions and execute them, leaving no stone unturned.

This is part of our daily prayer. By aligning ourselves and our realms to benefit from the resources God made available to the Redeemed, we have found that the yoke is much easier and the burden lighter than ever before (Matthew 11:28-30). Dr. Ron Horner would say, "Let the angels do the heavy lifting; you direct traffic." We feel better allowing the angels to do the heavy lifting since they excel at it!

> *Ask, and you shall receive. Seek, and you shall find. Knock, and the door will be opened unto you (Matthew 7:6-8)*

Chapter Thirteen

The Redeemed as a Praiser and a Hallelujah-Raiser

As I write this chapter, I am reminded of some of the lyrics of a song on Psalty's album—a Christian children's musical album— that I played frequently for my kids when they were toddlers: "I am a little praiser and a hallelujah-raiser, and I stand about three feet tall..."

When I read the book of Revelation, I see that singing praises to God is part of Heaven's culture, and it is loud singing (Revelation 5:11-14)! Thankfully, no one will have hearing issues in Heaven, and there will be no way to hurt anyone's ears with thunderous praise. Jesus taught us in The Lord's Prayer to request that the will of our Heavenly Father be done on earth as it is in Heaven. Therefore, replicating Heavenly praise sessions on earth is something the Redeemed get to do daily! I think God enjoys loud praises. I noticed during Jesus' time on earth,

He never rebuked anyone for praising Him loudly. In fact, He was pleased with it.

> *One of them, when he saw he was healed, came back, praising God in a loud voice. He threw himself at Jesus' feet and thanked him--and he was a Samaritan. (Luke 17:15-16)*

The Bible tells us that as Jesus rode on a donkey into Jerusalem, a crowd of disciples praised God *in loud voices* for all the miracles they had seen. This made the religious leaders mad and asked Jesus to rebuke His followers. Jesus informed the accusers that if the crowd kept quiet, then the stones would cry out!

> *When he came near the place where the road goes down the Mount of Olives, the whole crowd of disciples began joyfully to praise God in loud voices for all the miracles they had seen:*
>
> *"Blessed is the king who comes in the name of the Lord!" "Peace in heaven and glory in the highest!" Some of the Pharisees in the crowd said to Jesus, "Teacher, rebuke your disciples!" "I tell you," he replied, "if they keep quiet, the stones will cry out." (Luke 19:37-40)*

For the miracle of our redemption alone, no stone should ever have to cry out in our place. No cheering for a winning football team should be greater than the praises of the Redeemed. Singing praises and dancing before God has a way of recalibrating your whole being to resonate at Heaven's frequency. It also brings you into union with the divine nature. Not only is praise a weapon that binds the enemy, but it is also a double-edged sword that executes the sentence written against enemy forces (Psalm 149:3-9).

Worship, Praise and Thanksgiving

I have been asked the difference between worship, praise, and thanksgiving. Every act of obedience to God is worship. Praise is our worship for His ways—who He is. Thanksgiving focuses on His acts—what He does. The more you know His ways, the greater the depth of your praise. The more dependent you are upon Him, the more aware you are that apart from Him, you can do nothing (John 15:5), and the deeper your thanksgiving will be. Many have witnessed God's acts as Israel did, but few have sought to know His ways as Moses did (Psalm 103:7).

> *Enter into His gates with thanksgiving, And into His courts with praise. Be thankful to Him and bless His name. (Psalms 100:4 NKJV)*

When a person with a repentant heart approaches God with thanksgiving and praise, they are guaranteed to see God's salvation (Psalm 50:23). I believe the Father loves it when we commune with Him through worship. It is the way He prefers for us to engage Him. We are revitalized when we start recounting our blessings and His faithfulness. It reminds us of the greatness of the One we are approaching. It puts us in the right frame of mind to engage the all-knowing, all-powerful, and all-present God, the Holy One of Israel.

Unequalled Quality of Praise

There are certain sacrifices of praise and thanksgiving that no other created beings other than the Redeemed can offer to God. For instance, only the Redeemed can praise God and offer thanks for experiencing redemption. The angels observe our redemption, but they have not experienced it. Also, when you praise God for helping you as a parent, the holy angels can't offer that kind of praise because they've never experienced childbirth. When I chose to praise God when my son transitioned out of time, I was fully aware that I was presenting a sacrificial praise offering to God that no angel can offer because they have never experienced the loss of a child.

As the Redeemed, you will have many opportunities to offer the sacrifice of praise to God as you journey through time. Do not make light of such opportunities or pass on them. Your praises are prayers, and just as Cornelius's prayers in the Bible rose to God as a memorial offering (Acts 10:4), so do yours.

Through Jesus, therefore, let us continually offer to God a sacrifice of praise--the fruit of lips that confess his name. And do not forget to do good and to share with others, for with such sacrifices God is pleased. (Hebrews 13:15-16)

Fervency Counts

The Bible says, "The effectual fervent prayer of the righteous has great power and produces wonderful results" (James 5:16). God loves fervency in prayer, and thanksgiving and praise are both forms of prayer. To rephrase the scripture, the effectual fervent thanksgiving and praise of the righteous avails much.

People often ask me how I became fervent in thanksgiving and praise. My answer is that when you identify God as the source of who you are and all you have, you will not lack fervor in praise and thanksgiving. History with God produces passionate worship. When a song of praise or thanksgiving is being played, and you lack intensity in your response, this can be for several reasons. Perhaps you can't relate to the attributes of God that are being proclaimed. Maybe your love for Him has not yet risen above your needs and desires—like your need *not* to look weird, not to sound awkward, or to appear "dignified and normal," so to speak.

If God came through for you with a miracle when medical science had given up on you, I don't see how you can lack fervency in your response when you hear a declaration of His miracle-working power. If God took you from being nobody and made you somebody, I don't see how you would lack fervency in your praise when you hear a song declaring Him as the helper of the helpless. Can you see what I mean when I say your history with God produces zeal in worship?

The Judge Loves Songs

God loves to sing. Zephaniah 3:17 says, "He rejoices over us with singing." Pause for a minute and let this soak in. The I Am that I Am; the Ancient of Days; the Most High God; the One who has no beginning or end; the indescribable, uncontainable, unquestionable God; the God that robes Himself with fire as with a garment; the One whose throne is built upon righteousness and justice; the One who dwells in unapproachable light; the One who holds the winds in His hands; the God of all creation, sings over you with joy!

The first fruit of the Spirit listed in the Bible is love. God is love (1 John 4:8). The second is joy.

Singing and dancing are signs of a joy-filled spirit. Clothe yourself with this fruit as you approach God.

The Bible says, "With joy, you will draw water from the wells of salvation" (Isaiah 12:3). The joy of the Lord is your strength anytime, any day, anywhere (Nehemiah 8:10). Joy hurts Satan. Thanksgiving brings you through the gates; praise takes you into His courts.

As the Redeemed, you are called to be "a praiser and a hallelujah-raiser!" Some may say, *but I can praise God in my heart*. That is true. It should be normal to always have a glorious melody in your heart (Ephesians 5:19 KJV). However, there is a time to clap your hands and shout to God with a voice of triumph (Psalm 47:1 KJV). There is something about the shout of the Redeemed, as commanded by the Lord, which routes the enemy (2 Chronicles 20:22) and causes obstacles to crash like the walls of Jericho (Joshua 6:1-27). Do not be silent when you should be hollering unto God. Your "walls" just might be waiting to hear your shout.

Chapter Fourteen

Redeemed, But Who Am I?

I don't know everything there is to know about being the Redeemed of the Lord. I write as one who knows and prophesies in part (1 Corinthians 13:9). I am very thankful for the parts that have pleased our Heavenly Father to unveil to me. I know that if the Lord Jesus tarries, more mysteries will be revealed to each generation. As we journey through time, it is the glory of God to conceal a thing and that of kings to search things out (Proverbs 25:2). The Bible promises us that when completion comes, the parts will disappear. We shall know fully, even as we are known (1 Corinthians 13: 9-12).

Be All You Were Created For

Everything God allows in your life is about helping you become who you were created to be. Even allowing the devil to roam the earth from Genesis to Revelation is about you maximizing your God-given potential and receiving everything He wrote in Heaven's scrolls concerning you. Christian author and Bible teacher Kevin Zadai would say, "It's all rigged in your favor." You can't fail following the Holy Spirit. You have angels assigned to you that have no plan to fail and can't fail. All your Heavenly Father asks you to do is remain teachable and follow the Holy Spirit. If you don't know how I will tell you a secret: you can't miss Him following the Word.

As the Redeemed, I am:

- Fully known and accepted by God.
- A multidimensional, multifaceted spirit being having a human experience.
- Loved by the Father, Son, and Spirit of Holiness.
- Fearfully and wonderfully made.
- A called, chosen, unique bride of Christ in the making.
- Created to know Him, love Him, serve Him, and be happy with Him—both in this life and the life to come.
- Called to live as a foreigner and a nomad on earth and designed not to fit into a broken world.
- Called to a life of daily sanctification. Sanctification occurs when I lay myself on the altar of His Word and at the altar of the communion table.

- One given the privilege to know the secrets of the kingdom of Heaven.
- Designed to be dependent on God and interdependent on the body of Christ.
- Called to manifest Heaven daily as I journey through time.
- On earth, qualifying to rule and reign with Him, in and for all eternity.

Urgent Plea

I am honored that you read my book. If you enjoyed it, please take two minutes to leave a review on Amazon.com

Your feedback means the world and helps others discover it.

ANGELALOUGEE.COM/REVIEW

Thank you so much!

Sincerely,

Angela Lougee

Description

It's time to discover and exercise your full Kingdom rights and authority.

No man or institution can confer on you any honor greater than participating in time as The Redeemed of the Lord. But do you know who you are?

In *Redeemed, But Who Am I?* author and Bible teacher Angela Lougee uncovers in-depth, powerful, and life-changing biblical strategies to unlock the full rights, privileges, and benefits you are entitled to as the bride of Christ. If you are eager to know more about the Creator's sovereign plan for you, His incredible promises to you, and His supernatural power within you, accept this invitation to go on a journey through time and into the realm of eternity.

If you are tired of the shallow waters of lukewarm Christianity and want to dive deep into the heart of the mysteries of the kingdom of Heaven, this book will take you there and help you:

- Discover who you are as the Redeemed and why you are on earth.
- Find out how to experience a greater level of God's glory.
- Learn to exert authority over demonic forces and cast them out.
- See how to exercise your full kingdom rights and make room for more blessings.

Isn't it about time you enjoyed all the benefits Christ paid to give you?

About the Author

Missionary Angela Lougee is dedicated to disseminating practical biblical wisdom and imparting teachings to individuals striving to realize their divine purpose. She is a certified Behavioral Analyst and holds a Bachelor of Science in Microbiology, a Master of Business Administration, and a Master of Science in Human Resource Management from The Robert Gordon University in Aberdeen, Scotland.

Ordained as a Pastor and Life Coach, Angela demonstrates a fervent commitment to effecting positive transformations in the lives of others. With a wealth of speaking engagements across Africa, Europe, and the USA, Angela brings her profound insights and experiences to diverse audiences. Personally fulfilled by her marriage to Michael Lougee, they joyfully nurture a family of four children.

Published by:

A Division of LifeSpring Publishing
www.scrollpublishers.com

Has God spoken to you about writing a book?
Let us help you!

www.ingramcontent.com/pod-product-compliance
Lightning Source LLC
Chambersburg PA
CBHW031628160426
43196CB00006B/325